P9-CBL-295

Mangia with Micheline

A Journey of My Life Through Stories and Recipes
About Family, Friends and the Good Old Days

Micheline Grossi Lombardi

Mangia with Micheline

A Journey of My Life Through Stories and Recipes
About Family, Friends and the Good Old Days
By
Micheline Grossi Lombardi

Mangia with Micheline:
A Journey of My Life Through Stories and Recipes, About Family, Friends and the Good Old Days.
Copyright © 2015 Micheline Grossi Lombardi. Produced and printed by Stillwater River Publications. All rights reserved. Written and produced in the United States of America. This book may not be reproduced or sold in any form without the expressed, written permission of the author.
Visit our website at **www.StillwaterPress.com** for more information.
First Stillwater River Publications Edition
ISBN-10: 0-692-242303-6
ISBN-13: 978-069242303-5

Library of Congress Control Number: 2015932527

1 2 3 4 5 6 7 8 9 10
Written by Micheline Grossi Lombardi
All photographs property of the author. All rights reserved.
Some articles previously appeared in *The Foster Home Journal*, Foster, R.I..

Copyright © Micheline Grossi Lombardi.
Cover design by Jade Capobianco.
Cover photo by Kayla Salony of K. Salony Photography.
Published by Stillwater River Publications, Glocester, RI, USA.
Copyright © 2015 Micheline Grossi Lombardi.
All rights reserved.

Publisher's Cataloging-In-Publication Data
(Prepared by The Donohue Group, Inc.)

Lombardi, Micheline Grossi.
   Mangia with Micheline : a journey of my life : stories & recipes, family & friends, and the good old days by Micheline Grossi Lombardi.

   pages : illustrations ; cm

   "Some articles previously appeared in The Foster Home Journal, Foster, R.I."--Title page verso.
   Includes index.
   ISBN-13: 978-0-692-42303-5
   ISBN-10: 0-692-42303-6

   1. Lombardi, Micheline Grossi--Family. 2. Cooking, Italian. 3. Cooking, American. 4. Italian American families--New England. 5. Cookbooks. I. Title.

TX723 .L66 2015
641.5945   2015932527

DEDICATION

This book is dedicated to my mother, Mary Bevelaqua Grossi, my Grandmother, Michelina Iantosco Bevelaqua, and my Great Grandmother, Antonetta Tantimonico Iantosco. They shared the recipes, knowledge, and family values which shaped my life; also to Salvatore, my husband, the love of my life, who launched me on this new adventure.

ACKNOWLEDGMENTS

Many people made this book possible:

My husband, Sal Lombardi, who volunteered me to write a cooking column for a local monthly publication and encouraged me to spread my journalistic wings as well as my friends and family who offered recipes, stories, and encouragement.

Carol McCullough, the editor and publisher of the *Foster Home Journal* for including my stories. To my faithful readers in the towns of Foster, Scituate, Glocester, and Greene, Rhode Island, who so graciously praised my humble writings.

Barbara Stetson, the cookbook guru of Scituate, Rhode Island for sharing her experience, time and wonderful advice. Trisha Markman, my friend, who came to my rescue and took all my words and made it into a book. My sister, AnneMarie, my niece Tanya, and great niece Jade, for helping with the finishing touches. Helene Savicki, who edited my rambling style, and the many friends who added their suggestions and encouragements.

Most importantly, I owe my love of cooking to my grandmother, Michelina Iantosco Bevelaqua and my mother, Mary Bevelaqua Grossi. They taught me how to cook with love and intuition, by touch, feel, and often without measurements or a recipe.

INTRODUCTION

One day in 2006, I found myself writing a cooking column. My husband had volunteered my services to a local monthly publication! The idea intrigued me. It challenged me to develop a cooking column with a twist. This cookbook represents the journey of my life through stories and recipes. It's about family, friends, and traditions. It's about the role that food plays in the dynamics of my life, and maybe yours.

One of my first memories is sitting at my grandmother's kitchen table, playing with a little rope of dough, while my grandmothers made macaroni. I watched and learned to cook by touch, taste and intuition. While writing the column, I collaborated with my mother and aunt to hear stories from before my time.

Throughout my life I have dealt with difficult and frustrating tasks. Nothing to date can compare to the challenge of completing this cookbook. My niece Tanya informed me that I write like I talk and she undertook the chore of cleaning up my act, so to speak. As frustrating as this venture has been, it has also been enlightening, entertaining, and enjoyable to relive the stories and peruse the family photos. It was a joy to discover my family all over again. I hope you enjoy my tales through childhood and beyond to the present and the recipes that accompany them.

TABLE OF CONTENTS

2006 – The Beginning of "Mangia with Micheline"

2007 - Spreading My Journalistic Wings

2008 – Sharing Life Stories

2009 - The Challenge Continues

2010 - From Soup to Nuts

2011 – Something for Everyone

2012 – Sharing Family Traditions

2013 - Evoking Memories

Clockwise -Top Left: *November 18, 1940 - Joe Grossi & Mary Bevelaqua, Dad and Mom, on Borden St. in Providence.,* **Top Right**: *1950 - Uncle Leo and Aunt Rita Bevelaqua and me.* **Lower Right**: *Early 1940s - Uncle Joe Bevelaqua and my dad, Joe Grossi.* **Lower Left**: *September 1952 - My mother, Mary Bevelaqua Grossi, and grandmother, Michelina Iantosco Bevelaqua at the summer home in Bristol.* **Center**: *My baby picture.*

September 2006

Is It Gravy or Is It Sauce?

Growing up as a second generation Italian, I learned to cook at my grandmother and mother's sides in the old fashion way – "from scratch." My grandmother would give me family recipes, written half in Italian and half in English, with no measurements. She would say "add a little of this and a little of that and mix it until it feels right." I quickly learned when it "felt right," whether it was macaroni, meatballs, or cookies. Sunday was the day my mother would make the gravy for the macaroni. We always called it macaroni, not pasta.

I would wake up to the smell of sausage and meat browning in the pan before the tomatoes were added and then slow cooked for hours. It was a family tradition to have macaroni served with meatballs, sausage and braciola for our Sunday meal.

Now to the question of whether it is called gravy or sauce. In a glossary of Italian cooking terms, *sugo* is a sauce or gravy, when based on cooked meat; it is also called *ragu*, and is most often used with macaroni. On the other hand, tomato sauce is described as a red sauce, generally flavored with garlic and spices, served on pasta with shrimp. It is a light sauce.

So, when we brown sausage, pork, and beef to flavor the tomatoes, add tomato paste as a thickener and slow cook it, it is gravy. When we sauté garlic, spices, onions, then add tomatoes and quick cook it without adding a thickener, we call it sauce.

September 1964, Providence - My mom, Mary Bevelaqua Grossi, making Sunday Gravy.

How to Make Sunday Gravy

Ingredients:

1 to 2 tablespoons of olive oil
1 lb. Italian sausage (hot or sweet)
a piece of pork and or a piece of beef
4 garlic cloves, minced
1 tablespoon red pepper or to taste
1 cup red wine and water (fill cans of paste with water.)
6 fresh basil leaves, torn into small pieces
1 tablespoon fresh parsley, chopped into small pieces
3 cans (28-35 oz.) of Italian plum tomatoes
2 (6 oz.) cans of tomato paste
½ cup Pecorino Romano or Parmigiano cheese, grated

Kayleigh Bledsoe, my great great niece.

Method: Heat olive oil in a large heavy pot over medium heat. Pat the pork and beef dry and place in the pot. Add the sausage and cook until nicely browned on all sides, and crusty on the bottom of the pan. Add the garlic, and red pepper, then de-glaze the pan with either red wine or water, make sure you get all of the crusty meat drippings loose. (The leaner your sausage the less oil you will need.)

Puree the plum tomatoes in a blender with fresh basil and parsley and add to the pan, stirring to incorporate all of the drippings along with the grated cheese. Simmer over a low flame until the tomatoes start to darken, then add the tomato paste, with equal amounts of water and stir. Once the paste has dissolved, you can add the meatballs to the gravy and simmer over a low flame for several hours. (Stir the gravy every so often to make sure it is not sticking.)

October 2006

My mother, the oldest of eight, is 92 years young. She lives alone, and still cooks and bakes. Born in 1914, she was a young woman during the Great Depression. Having lived during that era, she learned to economize. To this day, she still washes out plastic bags, flattens out aluminum foil, and dries paper towels to use them over again.

November 1942 - My mom, Mary Bevelaqua Grossi on her honeymoon in New York.

Cooking nutritious meals for a large family on limited funds was a challenge since meat was at a premium. The meals we called "Mom's Depression Dishes" are now found on the menus of some of the best Italian restaurants. The weather is changing and the temperature is falling, so try my mother's "Depression Dish" with a crusty loaf of Italian bread.

Since I have never liked cannellini beans, I make Ceci e Pasta. It is the same recipe, but you substitute chickpeas instead. This soup can be served with an entrée or add a salad and make it a meal.

Pasta e Fagiole "Pasta and Beans"

3 tablespoons olive oil
1 medium onion, chopped
Crushed red pepper to taste
2 large cloves garlic, crushed
1 (28 oz.) can whole tomatoes, pureed
½ teaspoon salt
1 teaspoon basil
1 teaspoon parsley
½ teaspoon sugar
1 (19 oz.) can cannellini beans or ½ lb. cooked dried beans
1 cup cooked ditalini or other small macaroni, al dente
1 cup chicken broth, red wine or white wine (optional)

In a medium saucepan cook onions in oil until they are transparent, Add garlic and red pepper, and cook a few more minutes. Add tomatoes, salt, basil, parsley and sugar. Cook until tomatoes darken in color. Add approximately ½ to 1 cup of water, or chicken broth, or red wine to thin the sauce. Add the cannellini beans, drained to the sauce and simmer until beans are warmed. Just before serving, add the ditalini. Serve with grated Parmigiano or Romano Cheese.

September 1952 - Michelina Iantosco Bevelaqua (Grandma), and Antonetta Iantosco (Mamadona - Great Grandmother) in Grandma's kitchen on Borden Street.

November 2006

Sal, my husband of 27 years, ranks Italian restaurants on how they prepare his favorite dish, "veal saltimbocca." Saltimbocca is one of the classics of Roman cookery — a delicate dish as well as a hearty one. Careful cooking and good quality veal will give you a truly refined saltimbocca, which means, "Jump in the mouth."

He has sampled this entrée in restaurants in New York City, Boston, Rhode Island and anywhere we have traveled. He has asked me to prepare this dish for him on many occasions, but I have always declined, not wanting to disappoint him or receive a poor rating. It also seemed to be a lot of work to make it for just us. He finally broke me down and I decided to try my hand at making this recipe for our friends, Mike and Claudette Downey.

As usual, I looked at a few recipes, as the dish never had a consistent appearance from one restaurant to another; and I tried my own version. I served this dish with garlic-mashed potatoes and roasted asparagus. Sal said it was the best Saltimbocca he had ever eaten.

October 1979 - My husband Sal & me on our honeymoon cruise to Bermuda.

Veal Saltimbocca

Serves 6
1 ½ lbs. veal scaloppini, thinly sliced and pounded flat
12 fresh sage leaves, cut in half
12 very thin slices prosciutto (preferably Parma, it's worth the price)
12 slices of provolone cheese
6 tablespoons of unsalted butter
¼ cup dry white wine
¼ cup sweet Marsala wine
Flour for dredging
Fresh ground black pepper
4 tablespoons butter

Season the veal with pepper. Place 2 pieces of sage on each slice, then a slice of prosciutto, and then a slice of provolone, fold in half and secure with a toothpick. Pour about ½ cup of flour onto a piece of wax paper, and dredge the veal pieces in the flour, shaking off any excess.

Heat sauté pan over high heat, and add 2 tablespoons of butter to each. When the butter is hot, add the veal pieces and sauté until browned, approximately 2 to 3 minutes on each side. Remove to a platter.

Deglaze the pans by pouring half of the white wine and half of the Marsala wine into each pan and scraping the brown bits off the bottom of the pans. Then pour the liquid from one pan to the other. Cook until the liquid is reduced by about ⅓ (3 to 5 minutes). Reduce the heat; blend in the remaining 2 tablespoons butter, return the veal slices to the pan. Turn them over to coat in the sauce, and serve immediately.

1981 Woonsocket - My husband & me
lovey dovey crazy in love.

December 2006

Making cookies at Christmas time has been a tradition for as long as I can remember. The tradition dates back to my Great Grandmother, Antoinetta Iantosco and my Grandmother, Michelina Bevelaqua. My Grandmother would make cookie trays to give to the tradespeople who delivered the bread, soda, and mail, not to mention, all our relatives who came to visit.

I remember my mother baking cookies and my father helping her, or rather, my father putting in his two cents. He liked his cookies one size and my mother another! I remember my first Christmas in my very own apartment. There I was baking cookies, with Sal helping me, and suddenly I realized that "I *was* my mother."

I still bake cookies at the holidays and give trays away as gifts. One Christmas, I decided not to give trays to the family. All I can say is, it didn't go over very well! Of all my cookies, the Butterballs and Almond Slices are the most requested. Enjoy the cookies and make your own memories.

Butterballs (also called Christmas Nuggets)

2 cups sifted flour

½ teaspoon salt

¾ cup shortening

¼ cup butter or margarine

½ cup sifted confectioner's sugar

1 tablespoon vanilla

1 teaspoon almond extract

½ cup finely chopped nuts (I use pecans.)

Sift together flour and salt. Cream shortening, butter or margarine & sifted confectioner's sugar thoroughly. Blend vanilla, almond extract & nuts. (I use pecans) Add dry ingredients gradually; mixing until dough is smooth and well blended. Shape into small balls about the size of a walnut.

Place on cookie sheet and flatten slightly. Bake in slow oven (325°) 8 to 10 minutes. Do not over bake! Bake until just lightly browned. Roll warm cookies in confectioners' sugar.

You can also frost the cookies with chocolate and place Pecan halves on top.

Italian Almond Cookies

1 cup packed brown sugar
1 cup sugar
½ teaspoon cinnamon
⅓ cup oil
2 eggs

2 ½ cups flour
2 teaspoons baking powder
1 tablespoon water
½ lb. almonds (approx. 1 ¾ cups)
toasted, whole and chopped

Combine brown and white sugars, oil, and cinnamon. Add eggs and beat well. Sift flour and baking powder, and then add to the mixture. Add water and almonds. The dough will be thick and you may need to knead the almonds into the mixture. Shape dough into oblong loafs (dough will spread so not so wide or thick) on a greased cookie sheet and brush with a beaten egg.

Bake in a 375° oven for approx. 20 minutes until light brown in color. Cut into slices while warm. Place cut side down, return to oven, and bake an additional 5 minutes.

Iszabella Bailey,
my great great niece, making butterballs.

January 2007

The Christmas season is always the busiest time of the year for me. It seems as though I start cooking right after Thanksgiving and cook and bake nonstop until New Year's. I moved from my family home into my first apartment in 1977, after starting my very first professional job as a substance abuse counselor at the state's Adult Correctional Institution (ACI.)

I decided we should have a few friends over for a Christmas Party, and therein started the tradition of "The Party." After our marriage, our professional careers and outside interests expanded, as did our circle of friends and acquaintances. The party increased in size as our entertainment space increased.

So, for the last 30 years, we have hosted our party during the beginning of December and it has turned into a gala affair. I decorate the house, bake the cookies, make the food and prepare my special homemade eggnog. Once the party is over, I start baking cookies and making candy as gifts. Christmas Eve is our Open House, and of course more cooking. By the time that New Year's Eve rolls around, I am ready for a simpler way to entertain. A cocktail party with drinks and appetizers is just the thing.

So, I thought I would share a few of my favorite appetizer recipes with you. You can always buy marinated mushrooms at the store, but once you try the homemade kind, it's hard to go back to store bought.

Sal and Miki Lombardi going out to celebrate New Year's Eve.

Marinated Mushrooms

¾ cup olive oil

½ teaspoon parsley

⅓ cup balsamic or red wine vinegar

½ teaspoon oregano

1 ½ teaspoon salt

½ teaspoon hot red pepper flakes

¾ teaspoon sugar

2 bay leaves

½ teaspoon basil

1 or 2 garlic cloves, halved

⅛ teaspoon thyme

1 ½ lb. Mushrooms, halved if large

(I use Portobello mushrooms or a combination of white and Portobello)

In medium skillet, over medium heat, bring all the ingredients to a boil, except the mushrooms. Cover and simmer on low heat 10 minutes. Stir in mushrooms until coated, then cook over medium heat 3 to 5 minutes until the mushrooms are fork tender. Cover and refrigerate. When ready to serve, remove bay leaves and garlic, then drain.

Blue Cheese Ball

8 oz. Cream cheese

2 oz. Roquefort cheese, crumbled

2 tablespoons chopped celery

1 tablespoon minced onion

A few drops of Tabasco® sauce

Dash of cayenne pepper

¾ cup chopped pecans

Combine cheeses. Blend in next 4 ingredients. Chill for an hour, then shape into ball or log. Roll in chopped nuts to cover, chill. Serve the cheese ball at room temperature.

Velveeta® Cheese Ball

½ lb. Velveeta® Cheese

½ teaspoon salt

8 oz. Cream cheese

¾ cup chopped walnuts

½ teaspoon onion powder

2 teaspoons lemon juice

¼ teaspoon Garlic powder

1 tablespoon paprika

1 tablespoon chili powder

Soften cheeses and cut cream cheese into the Velveeta cheese. Add remaining ingredients and mix well. Shape into a ball. Roll in a mixture of 1 tablespoon chili powder and 1 tablespoon paprika, then refrigerate. Serve cheese ball at room temperature.

February 2007

February is here and it's time for Valentine's Day. Every year, I take out the wonderful heart shaped candy boxes that my father, Giuseppe (Joseph) Grossi, gave my mother in the 1940's to decorate my house. I remember almost every Valentine's Day, my father would bring home a box of chocolates for my mother. The funny thing was my mother really isn't that fond of chocolate, on the other hand, my father loved it. My sister, AnneMarie Grossi, and I have inherited the "chocoholic" gene from Dad.

So, between the two of us, we have tried many recipes. About 30 or so years ago, there was a recipe on a box of the pre-melted baking chocolate for a cake that seems like it would be tasty, so we tried it. My problem is I can never resist tweaking the ingredients to make it better. Sometimes it works and I improve the product and sometimes I go back to the original recipe. This time it is a winner!

After altering the original recipe, I present to you my all-time favorite and most requested chocolate cake. It is a very rich, dense, fudge cake with a layer of cream cheese weaving through the center. I frost the cake with a chocolate cream cheese frosting that makes it taste so good even frozen.

So, if you like chocolate, you will love my Fudge Ribbon Cake. Try it the next time you have a craving for a special treat.

1954 — Joe and Mary Grossi, my mom and dad. Mom sitting on Dad's lap and posing in the kitchen.

Fudge Ribbon Cake

Cheese Layer

4 tablespoons butter
2 eggs
16 oz. cream cheese
6 tablespoons milk
½ cup sugar
1 teaspoon vanilla extract
2 tablespoons cornstarch

Combine ingredients and beat at high speed until creamy, set aside.

Chocolate Layer

½ cup soft butter
2 cups flour
2 cups sugar
1-teaspoon salt
2 eggs
1 teaspoon baking powder
1 ⅓ cup milk
½ teaspoon baking soda
1 teaspoon vanilla extract
4 oz. melted unsweetened chocolate

Combine ingredients in large mixing bowl. Blend well; beat 4 minutes at medium speed. Spread half of the chocolate batter into a greased & floured 13 x 9 pan. Spoon the cheese mixture over the batter and top with the remaining batter spreading carefully to cover.

Bake at 350° oven (325° for glass pan) for 50 to 60 minutes or until cake springs back when lightly touched in center. Cool and frost with your favorite chocolate cream cheese frosting.

March 2007

March is here and spring is just around the corner. It is the month famous for the quote "Beware the Ides of March" which in the ancient Roman calendar is on the 15th of the month. Unfortunately for Julius Caesar, he forgot to beware! It is also the month that the Irish celebrate St. Patrick's Day (who by the way was a Roman) and the Italians celebrate St. Joseph's Day. Growing up, St. Joseph's Day was a special day in my family as both my father and brother are named Joseph.

Today, people associate the Zeppole pastry with St. Joseph's Day, but in my family, the tradition was to make doughboys. Of course, the Irish make Soda Bread. I have a wonderful recipe for Irish Bread that was given to me by my neighbor, Ann Lopardo, when we lived in Providence. Ann was Irish and her husband was Italian; they were a wonderful couple.

This is, by far, the best recipe for Irish Bread; it is moist and flavorful. I have changed the recipe just a little from the original and I never over-bake the bread, which will dry it out. So I present you with my favorite recipes for St. Patrick's and St. Joseph's Day.

Left: *My brother, Joe Grossi, at a family reunion.*
Right: *1976 — My dad, Joe Grossi, at his retirement party.*

Center:

Doughboys

Italian bread dough, fresh not frozen
Vegetable oil for frying

Dough will work better if it is at room temperature. Cut the dough into sticks, stretch out the dough the length you want and fry it in oil until golden. Drain on paper towels and sprinkle with sugar. You can also shake the doughboys in a plastic bag with sugar to coat them. Serve warm.

My great grand-niece, Iszabella, eating a dough boy.

Irish Bread

3 cups flour
1 cup sugar
3 teaspoons baking powder
1 teaspoon salt
3 tablespoons butter Crisco®, softened
1 ½ cups milk
1 cup raisins, immersed in whiskey (about a tablespoon)
2 teaspoons caraway seeds

Mix all dry ingredients together, cut in the Crisco® and then add the raisins, caraway seeds, and mix. Last add the milk and mix just until the mixture is moistened. Do not beat! Pour batter into a greased loaf pan, dab the top with butter and bake in a 350° oven for about 50 to 60 minutes. Let cool in pan 5 to 10 minutes.

April 2007

During the Easter season, it is a tradition for Italians to make rice pie and ricotta pie and for the last 30 or so years I have baked many. I learned to cook and bake prior to reaching my teenage years, but I was in my twenties before I attempted a pie. The pie crust looked really scary to make! I still remember my first venture into pie making. It was Easter. Sal was working for the Warwick Police department and telling his co-workers about Italian rice pie. Many of the police officers had never tasted a rice pie. Wasn't rice something that you fried, boiled and served with meat and vegetables… but in a pie?!

So before you knew it, Sal had volunteered me to make some pies to take into work. Of course, he failed to ask me if I could even make a pie! I was in a panic; I had never even attempted to make a piecrust, let alone a pie. However, I did have an ace in the hole, as my mother makes a great piecrust and had the recipe for the rice pie. I had a plan! I called my mother figuring I could get her to make the pies and I would get the credit. However, my mother had another idea. She would coach me on how to make the crust, but I would make it alone!

So that day, I made two rice and two ricotta pies and, in the process, I learned how to make a flaky piecrust. My mother always used the recipe that she found on a can of Crisco® to make crust. Whenever she made a rice, ricotta, or custard pie, she would substitute cold milk for the water in the recipe. I am including the piecrust chart (see Appendix for chart) as well as both recipes for my family's traditional rice and ricotta pie. I use the butter-flavored Crisco® when I make my crust. Both pies have only a single crust.

Easter 1980 — My sister-in-law, Anna Lombardi, and my mom, Mary Bevelaqua Grossi.

Italian Rice Pie

2 cups of cooked rice
1 cup of eggs
1 ½ cups of milk
¾ cup of sugar
½ cup ricotta cheese
1 can crushed pineapple, drained
¼ teaspoon cinnamon
¼ cup chopped cherries

Beat eggs with sugar, add all other ingredients and mix well. Pour into a prepared 10" unbaked pie crust. The filling comes up to the edge of the crust so I make a collar of foil around the pie to prevent the filling from spilling over. Bake the pie at 375° for 50 to 60 minutes. Note: I will also, towards the end of the baking, sprinkle chocolate jimmies on the top of the pie.

Ricotta Pie

1 ½ lbs. ricotta cheese
3 teaspoon cornstarch
3 eggs
1 teaspoon vanilla
¾ cup sugar
¾ cup mini chocolate chips

Preheat oven to 350° Blend all the ingredients together and pour into an unbaked 9" piecrust. Bake at 350° for 45 to 55 minutes.

Note: I sometimes use a teaspoon of Kahlua® or coffee flavored liquor in addition to the vanilla.

May 2007

  This coming October, Sal and I will be married for 28 years. For most of those years, I have come home from work, changed out of my suits and started supper. It has only been during the last few years that Sal has started to cook a meal for us. I have to tell you nothing beats coming home and being able to relax and not worry about cooking.

  It is wonderful to walk in the door on my late night to a well prepared meal. Sal would have opened a bottle of red zinfandel wine, the salad would be made, and the steak would be on the grill. Better yet, his special appetizer would be ready to serve.

  This month, I thought I would share his recipe for Portobello Mushrooms.

October 2004 — Sal and Miki Lombardi arrive in Brian Burke's 1949 Packard Station Sedan to renew their vows on their 25th anniversary.

Sal's Portobello Mushrooms

Pre-heat the broiler

1 Large Portobello Mushroom, per person
For each mushroom, you will need the following:
Olive oil
Crushed garlic
Thin slice of red onion
Slice of tomato
Thin slices of prosciutto (preferably Parma, it is worth the price)
Slices of provolone cheese

Brush the mushroom with olive oil and crushed garlic; add the onion. Place under the broiler and cook for 5 minutes. Next add the tomato, return to the broiler and cook another five minutes. Follow with the prosciutto and cook a few minutes. Last, top with provolone cheese and cook until the cheese is melted.

I hope you enjoy Sal's Portobello Mushrooms as much as I do.

July 2008 - Sal singing "Chantilly Lace in the Foster Idol at Foster Old Home Days.

June 2007

I started cooking before the age of six, due in part to my strong sense of survival and stubborn personality. One of my first memories is cooking Pastina with butter. I remember my mother had made Pasta e Fagiole "pasta and beans" for supper, a dish that to this day I will not eat. I really dislike eating beans especially cannellini beans. My father was from the "old school" the one that says you have to eat what was in your dish or you will be sent to bed without supper.

Even as a young child, I was just a wee bit headstrong. (Who would have ever guessed?) and I refused to eat my supper. My father was more headstrong than me, so off I went to bed without my supper. At that time and until the age of seven, my family lived downstairs from my grandparents, my great grandmother, and a couple of aunts and uncles in a wonderful extended family setting. After I was sent to bed without my supper, my parents went upstairs to visit my relatives. I decided I was hungry, remembered watching my mother make me Pastina, and thought I would try it.

So I found a pan and cooked myself my own dish of Pastina. Actually, I made Pastina several days in a row, because I kept being served the bowl of Pasta e Fagiole. Let me tell you, warmed over Pasta E Fagiole does not get better after a few days. That was my first foray into the field of cooking.

The first time I made a cake I was about 13 years old. It was a Wacky Cake (chocolate of course). This is a great cake for a kid to make because it is mixed all in one dish.

Of course, there is a story behind this adventure too. My parents and my Aunt Lottie and Uncle John Riccitelli had gone to the movies to see "It's a Mad, Mad, Mad, Mad World" and I was all alone in the house. While they were gone, I decided to try my hand at making this cake. Even then I was a night person and started baking before they returned from the movies. The cake had just come out of the oven, and I couldn't wait to try it. My mother for some reason believed that cake should not be eaten warm and since it was now close to my bedtime, I was told to wait.

So here was this wonderful cake, sitting there, with the aroma of chocolate in the air, and I was not allowed to even have a little piece. Mom said I had to wait because, "it will still be here in the morning." Now, I have an older brother, who had come home with his friend Billy, and the two of them ate the whole cake. I can tell you I was one disappointed girl! To this day, whenever I see Billy I remind him of the cake episode. So, here is my recipe for Wacky Cake. You can add chopped nuts, raisins, chocolate, butterscotch, or any other kind of candy bits to the batter for variety. I never frost the cake, but I do dust it with confectioners' sugar.

Wacky Cake

3 cups flour

2 cups sugar

6 tablespoons cocoa

2 teaspoons baking soda

1 teaspoon salt

1 teaspoon vanilla

⅔ cup oil

2 tablespoons white vinegar

2 cups water

Nuts, raisins or chips are optional

Confectioner's sugar for dusting

Sift all dry ingredients into a 13 x 9 baking pan.

Then make three wells. Into the first well put 1 teaspoon vanilla; in the second well add ⅔ cup oil; and in the last well add 2 tablespoons white vinegar. Pour 2 cups of water over the ingredients and mix. Bake the cake in a 350° oven for approximately 35 to 40 minutes. Dust the top with confectionery sugar. Nuts, raisins, or chips can be added if desired.

*Early 1960's — My brother, Joe Grossi, with his first car,
a 1953 candy apple red Ford on Beauford St. in Providence..*

July 2007

I work as a supervisor in Adult Probation and Parole at the RI Department of Corrections and recently I attended Training for Trainers with several of my fellow supervisors. We had to develop a lesson plan and make a presentation for the final class. Well, we all decided to have some fun and not have the presentations be work related.

With that in mind, Chrissy, being the mother of two young girls, decided to show the class how to make a paperclip/pencil holder. Crafts always come in handy when you have little kids. Nancy's presentation was how to fold an origami crane. Nancy was a brave soul since she had to learn to make the paper crane before she could teach the class. Shelley, after several changes in plans, decided to teach the correct way to plant a dahlia. Jessica, a new mother of a beautiful baby girl, decided her presentation was to show us the many ways to diaper a baby.

Since I love to cook, it seemed only natural that my presentation would be about food. Of course, the problem was how to have a cooking lesson without a kitchen, stove or all the ingredients on hand. I am famous for making the Italian version of an omelet a frittata. In fact, I have to make one each month for my morning staff meetings, otherwise the staff makes excuses not to attend.

OK, now I had the title of my lesson plan, but I still needed to figure out how to show people how to make one without having a kitchen at my disposal. My class-mates were all in agreement that I could bring in a cooked frittata, which we would dine on at the break. But that did not solve the problem of how to illustrate the process of making the frittata.

After many hours of thinking of one plan or another, I finally decided on pre-paring a PowerPoint presentation showing the various steps with the finished product being edible. I researched the internet for photos of ingredients and of course a frittata. I completed my lesson plan and the PowerPoint presentation, went shopping for all the ingredients, and paper plates with napkins to match and I was all set to go.

However all my plans went awry and the class never did get to eat breakfast. The day of the presentation I was ill and unable to go to work for several days, so I never did learn to make a pencil holder or fold a paper crane, plant a dahlia, or diaper a baby.

So, what follows is my basic recipe for a frittata. In an Italian home, food is always at the center of entertaining guests. The kitchen is the heart of the home.

A frittata is a meal that can be made with a variety of ingredients found in the refrigerator or pantry. It is easy to make and satisfying to the taste buds of the most discerning guest. A frittata is an Italian omelet that can be eaten either hot or cold. It can be a breakfast meal, a light lunch, and an appetizer or served as a light meal with a tossed salad. There are several ways to cook a frittata.

Frittata

Quantity of ingredients depends on the size of the pan.
Eggs, potatoes, onions, peppers, mushrooms, etc. (Be creative, any vegetable will work.)
Olive oil
Add to taste: garlic, parsley, pepper, Romano and Parmesan cheese

Directions:
Dice the potatoes, and chop onions and peppers
Clean and slice vegetables
Peel and crush garlic

To make the frittata, begin by setting the oven rack to the upper middle position and heating the oven to 400.° In an oven proof skillet (I use my cast iron pan) sauté the potatoes in olive oil until just beginning to soften. Add onions and cook until onions are translucent Add the peppers and sauté a few minutes. Add vegetables and garlic; sauté a few more minutes. While doing the filling ingredients, prepare the eggs and grate the cheese.

Lightly beat the eggs (about 2 eggs per person) to incorporate some air into them, which will make for a fluffier frittata. Add the Romano and Parmesan cheese, the ground pepper, and parsley.

Pour the egg mixture over the filling in the skillet and cook for a few minutes until the eggs set. Place the pan in the pre-heated oven and bake until eggs are puffed and set. It's ready to eat!

To take the frittata out of the pan, cut around the edges of the pan. Place a plate over the pan and flip the frittata onto the dish. Then flip over onto a second plate Cut into wedges and serve, hot, room temperature or cold.
If I'm making a small frittata, I use my 7" cast iron pan and cook everything on the stove. When the frittata is almost completely set, I place a plate over the pan and flip it onto the dish. Then I slide it back into the pan to finish cooking the other side.
I wish I could show you all the pretty pictures in my slideshow presentation. I hope that you will try making a frittata.

August 2007

Since 1977, Sal and I have hosted a party for our friends and relatives during the Christmas season. Each year the guest list grows proportionally with each new friend we make. It's easy to host a party if you make a phone call and have it catered, or if everyone helps by making a dish to bring to the party.

However, I'm just a little bit crazy and a bit of a control freak so I have to make everything myself. It's not as if I haven't tried to make it easier by hiring a caterer, but I'm always disappointed with the results. If friends offer to bring a dish, then I worry that they will be late, or not bring enough to feed everyone, or the flavors of the food will clash, or the plate they bring the food on will not match my table setting. So you can see my problem, I have to have control of the party.

As I have mentioned before I have followed the family tradition of making cookies and I usually make at least 15 different varieties for my trays. Cookies have always been what I serve as dessert at the party. Since, I make the cookies fresh; I will start baking about two weeks before the party. One year my sister, AnneMarie, convinced me to make desserts instead of the cookies for the party. It is so much easier to bake a cake than to make cookies. In fact, she even offered to help bake. AnneMarie is also a good cook and makes great desserts.

So that year, she made a pecan tart, a six topping cheesecake and I made the fudge ribbon and carrot cakes, just to name a few. The desserts looked wonderful and tasted great, but all night long people kept asking me where I was hiding the cookies. So, I'm back to making cookies.

In the February 2007 issue, I gave you the recipe for the Fudge Ribbon Cake so I thought you might like my carrot cake recipe.

Carrot Cake

2 cups sifted flour
2 teaspoons baking powder
1 ½ teaspoon baking soda
1 teaspoon salt
2 teaspoons cinnamon
4 eggs
1 ½ cups sugar
1 cup oil
1 can crushed pineapple (drained)
2 cups grated carrots
¾ cup chopped walnuts

August 1982 — Me with my birthday cake.

Sift dry ingredients, set aside. Beat eggs until lemon-colored. Gradually add sugar and continue beating. Add oil and beat well. Add dry ingredients, carrots, nuts, and pineapple. Mix well. Pour into greased and floured 13" X 9" pan. Bake in a 350° oven for 35- 44 minutes; 2 loaf pans for 50-60 minutes. Cool and frost with a cream cheese frosting, if desired.

Cream Cheese Frosting

8 oz. cream cheese, room temperature
1 teaspoon vanilla extract
½ cup butter, cut into pieces
1 lb. sifted confectioners' sugar

Beat cream cheese and vanilla until creamy. Gradually add butter, beating until incorporated. Gradually add the Confectioner's sugar, and beat until fluffy and smooth.

September 2007

My mother, Mary Bevelaqua Grossi, is a beautiful woman who wears her age well. The woman is unbelievable, her face is wrinkle free and her mind is sharp for her age. She turned 93 years old on January 15. The next day she was admitted into Kent County Hospital because she had a wound on her foot that was not healing. Every time a new nurse or doctor would come into her room to ask her questions to check her competency, they always did a double take and checked out her birth date. The woman does not look to be over the age of seventy.

My mother was in the hospital for 3 very long months; during her stay, she underwent two operations, one on the vein in her leg and the other to remove her toes. She was thrilled that both her surgeons were Italian. Due to her age, she was only given a spinal anesthetic so she was semi-awake during the operations. It was during the first operation that she heard her surgeon talking about how much he liked pepper biscuits, so as she tells it, "I piped right up and told him that I had a good recipe for pepper biscuits and that I would make him some."

My mother went home to her apartment after a month in rehab. It took her a little while to adjust to using a walker to get around, but she is back to cooking and baking. When she went to her first appointments after the surgery, she brought Dr. Lancellotti and Dr. Gallucci homemade pepper biscuits. She also makes great wine biscuits. I have included her recipes for both the wine and pepper biscuits. I hope that you enjoy them.

Pepper Biscuits

Dissolve one yeast cake in 1 cup warm water (temperature between 120°-130°) with 1 teaspoon of sugar in a 2 cup container, and let stand for a few minutes. Then add 1 cup of vegetable oil.

Sift together 5 cups of flour, 3 teaspoons of salt, 1 tablespoon of black pepper (fresh ground is best), and 1 tablespoon of crushed fennel seed. Make a well in the dry ingredients and add the liquid ingredients working into the dry mixture. Mix well and knead the dough for about 5 minutes. Cover and let rise until doubled in size. (About 1 ½ hours). Make into either sticks or round biscuits, wash with a beaten egg and bake in a 375° oven for approximately 30 minutes.

Red Wine Biscuits

½ cup oil
1-cup deep burgundy wine
½ cup Crisco®
1 cup of sugar
5 cups flour
5 teaspoons baking powder
1 beaten egg

Whisk together oil, Crisco®, wine and sugar. Set aside. Sift together flour and baking powder. Make a well, add the liquid ingredients, and mix well. Make into biscuits, wash with a beaten egg and bake in a 350° oven for approximately 30 to 35 minutes.

Easter 1980 — From left to right: My sister-in-law, Anna Lombardi, Me, and my mom, Mary Bevelaqua Grossi.

White Wine Biscuits

½ cup oil
1 cup white wine
½ cup Crisco®
1 cup of sugar, plus more
5 cups flour
5 teaspoons baking powder
2 tablespoons anise seed
1 beaten egg

Whisk together oil, Crisco®, wine and sugar. Set aside. Sift together flour and baking powder and anise seed. Make a well, add the liquid ingredients, and mix well. Make into biscuits, roll in sugar, wash with a beaten egg and bake in a 350° oven for approximately 30 to 35 minutes.

October 2007

Last month Sal and I attended the 140th Birthday Party for the YWCA of Greater Rhode Island. The YW is the third oldest YW in the United States, having been founded in 1867. Did you know that the YWCA founded Traveler's Aid, now known as Crossroads? Also, The International Institute, The Rape Crisis Center, now known as Day One, and The Blackstone Shelter, now the Blackstone Advocacy Center, just to name a few of the cutting edge programs founded by the YWCA throughout its 140 year history.

When I was about 14 years-old, my friend Arlene and I joined the YW Teens. It was a wonderful experience. Being a YW Teen brought me out of my shell, gave me self-confidence and empowered me to become the woman I am today. I was privileged to serve on the Board of Directors for ten years and was the President from 1997 until 2001.

You may be wondering what the story of the YWCA has to do with food. The year was 1964 and the YW-Teen Director, Cheryl Ann Hirst, decided that we were going to have an International Dinner for the immigrants at the International Institute. Another YW-Teen and I decided to make Eggplant Parmesan for about 50 people. What did we know about cooking for that many people and how time consuming making that dish really was? We must have fried about five large eggplants that day. Before we could start the project, we needed to buy the ingredients.

My mother taught me that eggplants are male and female. The male eggplants have fewer seeds, firmer texture and are less bitter. To determine the sex of the eggplant, you look at the blossom end and if there is a round dimple it is male, an oval dimple indicates it is a female. I recently checked the Internet to see if this was a correct way to determine the sex and learned that it is an old wives' tale, but my family has been using that method for years and I always seem to get the eggplants with the fewest seeds. So who really knows!

Eggplant Parmesan

Peel the eggplant and cut it into quarter-inch slices; salt them and layer them in a colander. Place a plate on top and weigh it down (a large can of tomatoes works well) to press out the bitter juices. After 1 to 2 hours rinse them and pat them dry. This method takes out the bitter juices. Then flour, egg, and bread each slice.

At this point, you can fry the eggplant in oil on the stove, which can take hours. If you are making a lot you can oven fry the eggplant. To oven fry, set oven to 375°/400°, put a thin layer of oil in a cookie sheet, place one layer of the eggplant, cook about five minutes, and turn over on the other side for another five minutes or until golden brown. Drain on paper towels.

To make the eggplant parmesan, you will need to layer the ingredients in a baking dish. You can use red gravy (meat based sauce) or a quick sauce (marinara).

Put a layer of the sauce, a layer of the eggplant, parmesan and mozzarella cheeses, and repeat until all the ingredients are used or the pan is full. Cover loosely with aluminum foil.

Bake in a 350° oven until hot and cheese is bubbly. In a 13 x 9 pan, it is about 45 minutes. Let it set for about 10 minutes before cutting.

Halloween — I was the gypsy trick or treating with all of the other neighborhood kids on Beaufort Street.

Purchasing Eggplant: *Smaller, immature eggplants are best. Full-size puffy ones may have hard seeds and can be bitter. Choose a firm, smooth-skinned eggplant that is heavy for its size; avoid those with soft or brown spots. Gently push with your thumb or forefinger. If the flesh gives slightly but then bounces back, it is ripe. If the indentation remains, it is overripe and the insides will be mushy.*

November 2007

On October 20th, Sal and I celebrated our 28th wedding anniversary and I was reflecting on how lucky I am to have found the man who is truly the love of my life. Throughout our lives, our paths have crossed, when we were kids, and again when we were teenagers, but it was not until we were in our twenties that we really met and fell in love.

As a very young girl, I used to go with my grandfather, Michele Bevelaqua, to Federal Hill to buy the grapes to make his wine. Was it really a coincidence or fate that the place where my grandfather brought his grapes was in the building owned by Sal's grandmother, Theresa Lombardi?

Sal and his sister Anna would stay with their grandmother, who lived upstairs, while his parents worked. Sal often helped the owner of the store at the same time I was with my grandfather picking out just the right grapes for the wine. I think it was fate!

Then again, as teenagers, our paths probably crossed at the S&S Dairy Treat in Johnston, where we went to socialize after the school day ended. We had friends and acquaintances in common. Sal even worked with my Uncle John Riccitelli. But it was not until that night at Allary's Jazz Club that I looked up and saw the man of my dreams, who is now the love of my life.

What does this story have to do with food, you might ask? Well, my beloved grandmother always said that the way to a man's heart is with a good meal. Of course, she said it in Italian! Once Sal tasted my cooking, he was hooked like it was Love Potion # 9!

Since it is November, I thought I would share a wonderful recipe for a squash and apple casserole.

Squash & Apple Casserole

The amount of ingredients will vary with the size of the casserole
Approximately 3 cups butternut squash, peeled and cut into 1" cubes.
3 to 4 apples, peeled and sliced. I always use a variety of apples like Gala, Granny Smiths, or Cortland.
½ cup brown sugar
½ cup chopped nuts (pecans work great)
1 teaspoon cinnamon
½ teaspoon nutmeg
¼ teaspoon cloves
butter to taste

Mix the sugar, nuts and spices together.

Layer the squash and apples, sprinkle with the mixture of sugar and nuts.

Dot with butter and repeat the layers until the casserole dish is filled.
Cover and bake in a 350° oven until apples and squash are cooked, approximately 45 to 60 minutes.

This is a great dish and you can control the amount of butter, spices and sugar to your taste. I am often asked to bring this dish to pot luck suppers. It's a side dish that tastes like a dessert.

1984 - Salvatore & Micheline Lombardi (My husband & me) dressed in 1940s attire on Longmont Street in Providence.

December 2007

Thanksgiving is over and I am starting to prepare for the Christmas festivities. It has often been said that I cook and bake nonstop from Thanksgiving until New Year's. It is so true! I have a "trim a tree" party (the secret of getting the tree trimmed with little effort), then our annual party, and finally an open house on Christmas Eve. I bake cookies and make candy to give as gifts and prepare the traditional recipes for Christmas Eve.

The Christmas season is my favorite time of year because it brings back all the childhood memories of family gatherings. In our family, Christmas Eve was the celebration. My aunts, uncles, and cousins would get together at my Grandparents' house and the meal would be a variety of fish dishes. There would be little necks on the half shell; Baccala (salt cod), shrimp and spaghetti, stuffed Calamari and fried smelts and of course Scungilli (snail) salad and that's just to name a few of the dishes. There would be cookies for dessert and then we would exchange gifts.

I make a number of the traditional fish dishes for the open house, but since we invite friends as well as family I also include dishes that do not include fish. Since I tend to cook the way my Grandmother taught me, which is by feel and taste without real measurements, the measurements are approximate.

December 1983 - Our Christmas tree on Longmont Street.

Scungilli Salad "Snail Salad"

1 lb. of partially cooked fresh or frozen Scungilli (conch or whelk meat)
1 tablespoon baking soda
Small red onion, sliced thin
Few stalks of celery, sliced
1 tablespoon fresh chopped Italian parsley
1 teaspoon fresh chopped basil
Juice and zest of one lemon
Crushed red pepper
Olive oil
Balsamic vinegar (or red wine vinegar)

Rinse the snails and place in a large pot of water with a tablespoon of baking soda. Bring to a boil, then simmer for about ten minutes. Although the snails are already cooked, this process will make the snails tender.

Rinse the snails in cold water and drain. Begin cutting the snails into ¼ inch slices. When you come to a dark tube filled with spongy matter, pull or cut it out and discard, as it can be gritty. The tube on the outside of the body does not need to be removed.

Place in a bowl. Add the celery, onions, Balsamic vinegar, olive oil, lemon juice & grated zest and spices to taste. Serve cold or at room temperature

---

Add your own twist...

Christmas Eve at our house.

Calamari Ripieni "Stuffed Calamari"

2 ½ lbs. cleaned large calamari (squid)
2 tablespoons olive oil
1 to 2 garlic clove, minced
½ cup plain bread crumbs
2 tablespoons chopped fresh flat-leaf parsley
2 tablespoons chopped black olives
2 to 3 chopped sun-dried tomatoes
3 tablespoons grated Romano cheese
Freshly ground black pepper

For the sauce:

¼ cup olive oil
1 large garlic clove, crushed
Small onion, chopped
½ cup dry red wine
2 cups chopped peeled tomatoes, with their juices (I use the blender to puree the tomatoes)
Crushed red pepper to taste

Wash the calamari under cool running water. Set the bodies aside. Chop the tentacles with a knife or in the food processor (they should be cut up fine, but not minced too small). All the ingredients should be chopped fine. Mix with a small spoons, stuff the bread crumb mixture into the calamari bodies. Do not fill them more then half-full. Pin the calamari closed with wooden toothpicks.

To make the sauce, choose a skillet large enough to hold all the calamari in a single layer. Pour in the olive oil and add the garlic and onions.

Cook over medium heat until garlic is golden and onions translucent. Add the calamari and cook, turning them gently, until they are just opaque, about 2 minutes on each side. Add the wine and bring to a simmer.

Stir in the tomatoes, crushed red pepper and salt to taste. Bring to a simmer. Partially cover the pan and cook for 50 to 60 minutes, turning the calamari occasionally, until they are very tender. You can add a little water or wine if the sauce gets too thick. Serve hot. Serves 6 to 8.

January 2008

Last November I told you how Sal and I met at Allary's Jazz Club and it was almost love at first sight. What I failed to mention was that he told me his name was Joe. Here was this six foot-tall man with a full beard, a full head of curly hair, a powder blue toke (knit hat) on his head, jeans and a T-shirt that said smoke Colombian. All I could see was his blue eyes and a grin that reminded me of a cat that ate the canary. Truthfully I was not impressed! I was with my sister, AnneMarie, that night and I told her that there was something just not right with this guy.

A few weeks later, I met him again at a friend's party and someone called him Sal. Now I was really suspicious! I suspected that he was a cop and I was right. During the first few months that I knew Sal, he had a few names, first it was Joe and then it was Andy and finally it was Frank. He had graduated from drugs to stolen goods.

When Sal and I were married in 1979, he was involved in an undercover sting operation in Woonsocket. His name was Frank Torro and I was his moll (girlfriend), Miki Grossi. Since Woonsocket was a close knit community, it was important that I be identified as his girlfriend for the sting operation to be successful.

We rented a wonderful apartment on the first floor of a Victorian house called the I.M.Bull Mansion under our aliases. Frank would drive me to our landlord's house in a 1979 black Cadillac and I would pay the $500 rent in one hundred dollars bills. His cover was that he was an antique dealer, who would buy whatever you had to sell. The image we projected was of a gangster, who likes to live the good life.

So here I was a newlywed, unable to change my name, living with a man I had to call Frank, and pretending I was a gangster's moll. I also went on dates with Frank and his newfound friends who were later arrested for trafficking in stolen goods.

Additionally, we entertained Frank's friends in our apartment. That first New Year's Eve we had a party for a few of "our friends." I served chicken piccata with capers, oven-roasted potatoes, and sautéed escarole. Here are the recipes for chicken piccata (which means with a bite) and sautéed escarole.

Chicken Piccata with Capers

1 lb. chicken cutlets
Salt and freshly ground pepper
¼ cup flour
2 tablespoons unsalted butter
1 tablespoons olive oil

½ cup chicken broth
2 tablespoons rinsed capers
1 tablespoon fresh lemon juice
1 tablespoon chopped fresh flat-leaf parsley

Place the chicken between two sheets of plastic wrap and with a meat mallet, pound to ¼ inch thickness. Sprinkle the chicken with salt and pepper. Spread the flour on a plate and dredge the cutlets in the flour and shake off the excess. Melt 1 tablespoon of butter with the olive oil in a large skillet over medium heat. Add the chicken to the pan and brown the cutlets on both sides. Only place in the pan, the number of cutlets that will fit without crowding. Transfer them to a plate and keep warm. Repeat with the remaining chicken.

When all the cutlets are browned, pour the chicken broth into the pan, cook at high heat, scraping the bottom of the pan, until all the liquid is slightly thickened. Stir in the capers, lemon juice, and parsley.

Remove from the heat and swirl in the remaining tablespoon of butter. Pour sauce over the chicken and serve immediately. Garnish with thin slices of lemon.

You can also make this dish with veal, fish fillets, or thin slices of pork cutlets. Serves 4.

1980 - Sal as Frank Torro in our apartment in the I.M.Bull Mansion in Woonsocket.

"Frank" and his moll dressed for a night on the town.

Sautéed Escarole with Garlic

1 head of escarole
3 garlic cloves, crushed
4 tablespoons olive oil
2 tablespoons white wine
Crushed red pepper to taste

Trim the escarole and discard any bruised leaves. Cut off the stem ends. Cut the leaves into bite-sized pieces.

In a large skillet, cook the red pepper and garlic in the olive oil over medium heat until the garlic is golden. Make sure the garlic doesn't burn.

Add the escarole, stir well and cover the skillet until the escarole is wilted. Once it is wilted add the white wine and more olive oil if needed. Cook until escarole is tender. Serve hot or room temperature. Serves 4.

Left: *1980 - Sal as Frank Torro in our apartment in the I.M.Bull Mansion in Woonsocket.* *Below:* *As Frank Torro hanging out at Antique Brokers.*

February 2008

Thirty years ago this month was the Blizzard of 1978. It had started out as an ordinary workday. I was working as a drug counselor at the ACI for TASC (Treatment Alternatives to Street Crime) and Sal was working a storefront undercover operation in Woonsocket. (Frank's Second Hand Shop. His motto was "I'll buy anything you can't sell").

Several of my co-workers and I had gone out to lunch to celebrate a birthday at Twin Oaks, it was not snowing when we left the office. Within the hour that we were at the restaurant, the snow had begun and by the time we got back to the office the snow was really coming down. The office closed down about 1:30 p.m. and I started home to our apartment in Pawtucket. It took me about two hours to make the 20 minute ride home.

I called Sal and urged him to come home right away as the weather was getting really bad. The snow kept coming. Sal left Woonsocket about 3:00 PM and since it was the days before cell phones, he would call me periodically along the way. It took him over five hours to make the trip home. He had managed to drive the car almost all the way home, but he had to leave it at the intersection of Main Street and Lonsdale Avenue right in front of the New York Lace Store. He walked the rest of the way to the apartment, which was about two blocks. He looked like the abominable snowman, covered with snow and half frozen, but he had made it home!

Since I wasn't sure when he would make it home and I knew he would be cold and hungry I had decided to make one of my favorite meals, lentil and rice. There is nothing better than soup for cold weather. My family always makes lentils and rice and Sal's family makes lentils with pasta. Lentils represent good luck in Italy and are traditionally eaten in one form or another on New Year's Day.

If you want Sal's version, instead of rice, add cooked small macaroni like ditalini.

Lentils & Rice Soup

½ lb. of dry lentils, washed
2 or 3 bay leaves
3 garlic cloves, chopped
1 small yellow onion, chopped
2 carrots, chopped
1 celery stalk, chopped
Red pepper flakes, parsley, and basil to taste
Olive oil
15 oz. can of tomatoes, pureed
Rice, cooked

Place lentils in a 4 qt. saucepan, cover with water, add bay leaves, and one clove of garlic. Cook until the lentils are soft, but not too soft. Lower heat and simmer for 25 to 30 minutes, keeping the level of the liquid just over the lentils by periodically adding hot water. Season with salt and pepper to taste.

In another saucepan, sauté the onions, garlic, carrots, and celery until the vegetables are softened. Add the tomatoes and cook until the tomatoes turn darker in color. Add the tomatoes to the lentils. Add red pepper flakes, fresh or dry parsley and basil to taste. When ready to serve add the cooked rice to the consistency you prefer.

Serve with grated Parmigiano cheese and Italian bread.

Note: If using dry herbs, use less than if you use fresh herbs.

My great-great-niece, Iszabella Bailey,
as a snow bear going out in the snow
for her first blizzard

March 2008

I'm a city girl, having grown up in Providence. Sal is a country boy having grown up in Johnston, when the town was as rural as Scituate and Foster. As I have mentioned before, Sal was an undercover detective working in narcotics when we met and I was not aware of his interest in country life.

As our relationship grew and we shared more about ourselves, I learned about his experiences living in the country. He talked about joining the 4-H when he was 14 years old and what a wonderful experience it was for him.

He raised Dutch Rabbits, Phoenix and Silkie poultry and grew vegetables. He entered his animals and vegetables in competition for ribbons at the Foster and Rocky Hill fairs.

I, on the other hand, had never heard of the 4-H, had never seen a chicken up close and personal, and had never been to the fair.

That is, of course, until I met and married Sal Lombardi. I can only say that you haven't lived until you have given a live chicken a bath in your kitchen sink so they can look all pretty for a poultry show!

When we moved to Scituate, Sal decided that he wanted to go back to his country roots and raise chickens, not just any chickens, but fancy chickens. So, he built a coop and purchased some Silkie and Phoenix poultry. Silkies have purple skin, feathered legs, and feathers on their head that look like they are wearing a hat. The feathers look like fur and they waddle when they walk. They remind me of Smurfs. The Phoenix roosters have tails that grow very, very long. These are not your normal chickens. We had to take pictures of them, so that my mother could show all her friends at the Senior Center, what her "grandchickens" looked like.

The first Easter we had the chickens, I colored their eggs. Since they are Bantam poultry, the eggs are smaller than the store bought kind. My mother thought they looked "cute", and they are just the right size for kids.

Last year I shared my recipes for rice and ricotta pies that we traditionally make for Easter. This month, I thought I would share another Easter pie specialty called pizza gain or pizza rustica. This recipe serve 8 to 10 people.

Pizza Rustica

Dough
4 cups flour
1 ½ teaspoons salt
½ cup Crisco® shortening
8 tablespoons unsalted butter, cut in pieces
2 large eggs, beaten

Combine the flour and salt in a food processor. Add the shortening and butter and pulse until the mixture resembles large crumbs. Add eggs, pulse briefly until the ingredients come together and form a soft dough.

If the dough seems too dry and crumbly, add a little ice water. Don't over-mix, or the dough will be tough. Shape one-third of the dough into a disk. Make a second disk with the remaining dough. Wrap each piece in plastic wrap. Refrigerate at least 1 hour.

Filling
2 lbs. ricotta cheese
4 large eggs, lightly beaten
1 cup grated Romano cheese
½ teaspoon ground pepper
4 oz. of prosciutto, chopped
4 oz. sliced salami, chopped
4 oz. sliced peppered ham, chopped
2 tablespoons chopped fresh Italian parsley
1 egg yolk, beaten with 1 tablespoon water

To make the filling: In a large bowl, beat the ricotta, eggs, grated cheese, and pepper until well blended. Stir in the chopped cheese, meats, and parsley.

DIRECTIONS:
Preheat the oven to 375° On a lightly floured surface, with a floured rolling pin, roll out the large piece of dough to a 15-inch circle. Drape the dough over the rolling pin.

Transfer the dough into a 9 x 3 inch spring form pan, flattening out any wrinkles against the inside of the pan. Pour the filling into the pan.

1995 - **Left:** *Silkie rooster.* **Below:** *Phoenix rooster.* **Right page:** *Japanese Silkie rooster and hen..*

Roll out the remaining dough into a 9 inch circle. Cut the dough into ½ inch wide strips. Place half of the strips 1 inch apart over the filling. Turn the pan clock wise and place the remaining strips on the top, forming a lattice pattern. Pinch the edges of the strips and bottom layer of the dough together to seal. Brush the dough with the beaten egg.

Bake the pie 1 to 1 ¼ hours, or until the crust is golden and the filling is puffed and set in the center. Cool the pie in the pan on a wire rack for 10 minutes. Remove the sides of the pan and cool completely. Serve at room temperature or lightly chilled. You can store it in the refrigerator, covered up to 3 days.

I have made a version of this pie using fresh basket cheese instead of the ricotta, with cooked crumbled hot sausage, asparagus, and veal. You really can use any kind of cooked meat and cheese.

Add your own twist...

April 2008

It's funny how an event can trigger a thought that can send you on a trip down memory lane. Last month, I was in the mood to make some liquors to have on hand for gifts. In looking over my recipes, I came across a hand written recipe card for Annie's Bailey's® Irish Cream.

So instead of making the liquor, I just had to call and talk with my friend and reminisce. I met Anne Laliberte, when Sal and I lived in Woonsocket during the undercover sting operation. Anne owned a club called "Poor Annie's", where Frank Torro (AKA Sal Lombardi) and his "girlfriend" Miki Grossi would go for a few drinks. I really liked Anne, but due to the fact that Sal was undercover, I wasn't really able to foster a friendship. Let's face it, Anne believed that Frank Torro was a gangster and that I was his "moll." Before the undercover operation was over, Anne had decided to move to Florida, so I thought that I had lost my chance at this friendship. Well it's really funny how life works sometimes because our paths crossed again.

Frank Torro would also frequent antique stores in his quest for stolen merchandise. It was at Antique Brokers that he made friends with Gerry Tucker, a legitimate dealer. The morning that the sting operation was going down and the criminals were being rounded up and arrested, I was busy setting the record straight with a few people. My first stop was to our landlord's to explain that they weren't really renting to a mobster, but to a cop. My second stop was to Antique Brokers to reintroduce myself to Gerry. Needless to say, Gerry became a friend.

Anne came back to Woonsocket for her brother's wedding and met Gerry and started dating. It was during this time that Gerry discovered that Sal and I knew Anne, but as Frank and Miki. So, he decided to bring her to our house for dinner, but he told her she needed to be blindfolded because he was taking her to a secret location.

What a surprise when I answered the door and there was Poor Annie! We became good friends, but it did take a while for her to remember to call my husband, Sal, and not Frank.

So here is the recipe that inspired my trip down memory lane.

Annie's Bailey's® Irish Cream

2 to 3 cups Irish Whiskey
3 cans sweeten condensed milk
1 dozen eggs
1 quart half & half
2 tablespoons Hershey® chocolate syrup
1 teaspoon almond extract

Blend together, and put into sterilized bottles and refrigerate.
Let sit for two weeks, shake before serving. Best served cold.

Anne Laliberte and Gerry Tucker. Our friends in Florida who originally met "Frank and Miki."

May 2008

Last month Sal and I attended the Scituate Financial Town Meeting. Since I grew up in Providence, attending town meetings was an experience that was new and different when we moved to rural America. I was brought up to believe that voting was a privilege and a duty and I have never missed an election since I was old enough to vote. I thoroughly enjoy the drama and passion of the people who attend the town meetings and make their voice known. It truly is America at its best. However, it continues to amaze me that so few citizens attend to vote on the future of their town.

Anyway, while I was there, I saw Police Chief Bill Mack and his wife Paulette. It triggered a memory and, of course, a recipe. Bill and my husband were on the Woonsocket Police Department together and they share a love for antique cars. I would see Bill and Paulette on the antique car show circuit during the years and we would chat. At most, we were acquaintances that shared common interests. When Bill was hired as the police chief, they decided to move from Woonsocket to Scituate.

Having relocated to Scituate only a few years before, I remember how hectic it was to move and then to even think about having a meal. So I called Paulette and confirmed their moving date and told her not to worry about supper that night. After work, I came home and cooked grilled chicken salad, macaroni salad (I never call it Pasta, it will always be macaroni to me), a string bean salad, and brownies. I packed a picnic basket and drove over to their new home with supper for them.

Since that time, we have shared many a meal and at Christmas I always give them a tray of cookies, with Bill's favorite brownies (October 2010.) So here is my recipe for grilled chicken salad. I hope you enjoy the chicken and remember that anyone who is moving would enjoy a picnic meal.

Grilled Marinated Chicken Salad

Boneless chicken breasts
Portabella mushrooms
Red, orange, and yellow peppers
Good Seasons® Roasted Garlic salad dressing made with olive oil and balsamic vinegar.

Brush the dressing over the chicken and grill until done. Brush the dressing over the mushrooms and grill. You can either grill the peppers the same way or serve them raw. After the chicken and mushrooms are cooked, slice the breasts and mushrooms, add the peppers and drizzle balsamic vinegar over the top. Serve warm.

A 1951 Lincoln Cosmopolitan looking pretty on the beach.

Add your own twist...

June 2008

I started thinking about vegetable gardens the other day and how they have always been a part of my life as well as my husband's. My thoughts were triggered by Sal's traditional mother's day present of tomato plants. My mother-in-law, Anna Loffredo Lombardi, loves to work in the garden, both planting flowers and vegetables. Sal, as a teenager in the 4-H club, grew vegetables and entered them in the local fairs, often winning ribbons for his efforts.

When I was growing up, my grandfather, Michele Bevelaqua had a wonderful vegetable garden and he taught me many things about growing vegetables. For instance, I know that you should plant marigolds around your tomato plants to prevent the insects from killing the plant. I remember my mother telling me that everyone had a "victory garden" during World War II in order to supplement the family's food rations.

My father planted a garden for years, growing tomatoes, zucchini, peppers, Swiss chard, and herbs. There is nothing like going in the garden and picking fresh vegetables for your meal. I am trying to convince Sal to go back to his 4-H experience and plant a few vegetables this year. Considering the high cost of food; maybe it's not a bad idea to go back to those victory gardens.

Although, my grandfather taught me about the growing ends of a garden, my grandmother taught me how to cook all those wonderful vegetables. One of my father's favorite, all-time fresh, out-of -the- garden treats was a fried zucchini flower, picked first thing in the morning. I am sure many of you are thinking how do you eat a zucchini flower, others wanted to know why in the world you would eat a zucchini flower. Because they really are quite wonderful, here is the recipe for those adventurous readers out there in rural Rhode Island

Fiori Zucca Fritti "Fried Zucchini Flowers"

⅓ cup flour
⅓ cup cornstarch
½ teaspoon salt
Freshly ground pepper
½ cup sparkling mineral water
Vegetable oil for deep-frying
16 zucchini or other squash blossoms

In a small bowl, whisk together the flour, cornstarch, ½ teaspoon salt, and pepper to taste. Stir in the water. Let stand for 1 hour.

Pour 2 inches of oil into a deep fryer or deep heavy saucepan. Heat over medium heat until temperature reaches 375° on a thermometer or when a drop of the batter sizzles and quickly rises to the surface of the oil.

Dip a zucchini flower in the batter, coating it completely. Slip into the oil. Dip and add as many flowers as will fit without crowding them in the pan. Fry turning once, for 1 to 2 minutes until crisp. Remove the flowers and drain on paper towels and serve immediately. You can also add a small piece a cheese into the flower before you dip them in batter. Serves 4.

September 1952 - Michele Bevelaqua, my grandfather, preparing the garden at our summer home in Bristol.

July 2008

As I have mentioned before, I met my husband at a jazz club in Providence in 1976 when he was working as an undercover police officer. His job at the time was to arrest drug dealers. He certainly looked the part of a "drug user," with his long hair and wearing jeans, sneakers, and his famous t-shirt that said "Smoke Colombian." He also drove an old car, a 1947 Packard. Who knew what a Packard was, certainly not me! It was a car that I had never heard of before I met him. Well in the last 32 years that we have been together, I have discovered there are many automobiles that are rare and unusual.

Sal has a passion for antique cars and we have had a few over the years. Throughout the years we have owned the 1947 Packard Clipper, a 1937 Cadillac, a 1954 Buick Skylark, a 1951 Lincoln Cosmopolitan, a 1954 Hudson Hollywood Hornet (big and red and lots of chrome!), and my first very own antique car, a 1956 star mist blue Thunderbird… just a few of the highlights. Sal gave me the Thunderbird for my birthday in 1995.

Driving in an antique car is like being in your own parade. People look at you and wave, they beep their horn, and the children look with their eyes wide, wondering about these strange vehicles driving down the street.

We often drive to antique car shows both in Rhode Island and other states in New England. Some car shows have contests in addition to having the cars judged and winning a trophy. We once won third place in Stowe, Vermont for having the correct outfit to match the era of the car. Since we had driven a pre-World War II car, we had dressed in military uniforms; I was a Tech Sergeant and Sal a pilot.

We have also participated in the tailgate picnic contests. We have a picnic case with dishes, silverware, thermos and a folding table for four.

You are judged both on the best display of items that match the car and the food on display. People will go all out, displaying an elaborate picnic with wineglasses, cheese, a variety of different foods, music of the era playing, and maybe a magazine or two from the past. I have a World War II Women's Army Air Corp Tech Sergeant uniform for the pre-war cars, a fifties felt skirt, and a duster for the Model T.

Last month, we drove our 1941 Cadillac 60 Special with wood trim to Manchester, Vermont and stayed at a beautiful Inn overlooking the mountain. The Manchester Show ends up on Father's Day every few years, so we ended up missing one of my all-time favorite shows at the Portsmouth Abbey in Portsmouth, Rhode Island.

I always pack a picnic lunch with enough food to feed the small army of friends that visited the show. They always want to know if I have made my Italian macaroni salad, so I thought I would share the recipe.

Italian Macaroni Salad

1 package of tri-color rotini macaroni
1 package of the fresh very small cheese ravioli
1 can chick peas (ceci beans), rinsed and drained
Yellow, orange, and red peppers, diced
Black and/or green olives, sliced
1 carrot, grated
Marinated artichoke hearts and/or mushrooms
Celery
Red or Spanish onion sliced
Pepperoncini peppers, sliced
Broccoli, asparagus or green beans – al dente and sliced
Grated or shredded parmesan or romano cheese
Virgin olive oil
White balsamic vinegar
1 package of Good Seasons® dressing
Garlic, parsley, basil, and pepper to taste

Cook the rotini until al dente, adding the ravioli a few minutes prior to the rotini's completion time. The ravioli will only need to be cooked for a few minutes, as it is fresh. DO NOT OVER COOK the macaroni, as it needs to be al dente.

While the macaroni is cooking, slice and dice the vegetables, quarter the artichoke hearts and mushrooms; steam the vegetables and slice. Mix the oil, vinegar, and Good Seasons® salad dressing in a blender and mix well. Mixing it in the blender will keep the dressing from separating. You can use whatever white vinegar you like if you can 't find white balsamic.

Once the macaroni is done, drained and rinsed, add it to a large bowl and pour on some of the dressing. Add the other ingredients and spices and cheese to taste. The salad can be served room temperature or chilled. I will vary the ingredients based on whatever I have on hand. I try to make it colorful and add different vegetables for variety. I hope you will try this dish at your next picnic. The amount of ingredients will vary depending on how many people you are planning to feed.

Above and opposite page: *2008 - Sal & Miki dressed in our World War II uniforms in front of the 1941 Cadillac at an antique car show in Stowe, Vermont.*

Add your own twist...

August 2008

I was born on a Thursday in August a number of years ago. In fact, my father, mother and brother were all born on Thursdays. I always thought it must be somewhat significant we were all Thursday babies. I remember a superstitious rhyme which predicts the personality of a child. It goes something like "Thursday's child has far to go" or if you prefer the 1887 version "Thursday's child works hard for a living." Now that saying seems to fit!

Anyway, as I am approaching another birthday, I started to think about the difference between my generation and the younger generation (OH, God did I really say that!) as it relates to birthday parties.

Growing up, my family celebrated our birthdays with my mother making our favorite cake. Rarely did we have a party with friends or even with all the related aunts, uncles and numerous cousins.

Now-a-days, parents throw their kids theme parties with entertainment, pony rides, magicians and maybe an appearance by the Cookie Monster.

The first year that Sal and I were together, he planned a surprise party for me. We had gone to Cape Cod for a few days and on the way back home, he suggested that we stop by my sister's house. Little did I know he had arranged for my sister to host the party and he had invited all my close friends. He also asked her to make my favorite cake.

November 1995 - Driving my 45th birthday gift from my loving husband in the Scituate Veteran's Day parade.

No one had ever given me a surprise party before and his gesture touched my heart and made me love him all the more.

Over the years, Sal has surprised me with many beautiful presents both for my birthday and for no particular reason other than he knew the outfit would look good on me.

One of the most memorable gifts was a star mist blue 1956 Thunderbird, a gift for my 45th birthday. The T-Bird was on my wish list of most desirable cars. I remember that right after the T-Bird arrived in our driveway, I took it for a spin around town. It was on a Sunday afternoon and I decided to go to the IGA to pick up a few things.

When I pulled into the parking lot of the IGA, there were just a few cars in the parking lot. However, 15 minutes later I left the store and there were guys surrounding the T-Bird. The car was a guy magnet!

Over the years, I have received many presents, but I will never forget that surprise party. It just confirmed what a special man my husband is to me. My friends all want to know if he can be cloned.

One of the birthday cakes I remember my mother baking was the chocolate speckled chiffon cake.

Above: *Summer 1990 - Me vacationing in Nantucket during the daffodil festival.*

August 1954 - My dad, Joe Grossi, in our kitchen on Borden Street at my 4th birthday.
The chocolate speckled chiffon cake is in the foreground

Add your own twist...

Chocolate Speckled Chiffon Cake

1 cup egg whites, at room temperature (7 or 8 eggs)
½ teaspoon cream of tartar
1 ¾ cups sugar
2 ¼ cups cake flour
1 tablespoon baking powder
1 teaspoon salt
½ cup salad oil
5 egg yolks
¾ cup cold water
2 teaspoons vanilla extract
4 squares bittersweet chocolate, grated

In large bowl with mixer at high speed, beat egg whites with cream of tartar until soft peaks form; beating at high speed, gradually sprinkle in ½ cup sugar, a little at a time, beat until sugar is completely dissolved. Whites should stand in stiff peaks. Do not scape bowl during beating.

In another bowl, with mixer on low speed, beat flour, salt, baking powder, 1 ¼ cups sugar, cold water, oil egg yolks and vanilla extract until blended. Beat at medium speed until smooth, scraping bowl often. Fold in grated chocolate; then gently fold mixture into the egg whites. Pour batter into an ungreased 10 inch tube pan and bake 60 to 65 minutes at 350 until top springs back when lightly touched with finger. Invert cake on bottle to cool completely. With spatula, loosen cake from pan and invert on plate. Frost with your favorite chocolate frosting.

September 2008

It's funny that, growing up, I thought country life would be boring. After all, being a city girl, I was used to being able to hop a bus and go "down city" shopping, walking down the block to the grocery store, and (oh my God) walking to school. The city has restaurants, movies, shops, and theaters. I mean what's there to do in the country?

Well let me give you a little snapshot of what Sal and I did in the month of August. The first Sunday in August, the Greene Public Library hosts a chicken barbecue fundraiser. The price is right at $8.00 per person, the location picturesque and the food wonderful.

The menu includes homemade potato salad, tossed salad, coleslaw, baked beans, homegrown garden tomatoes, macaroni salads, and desserts. We have been attending this event for the past several years. We always get contacted with the date of the barbecue.

This year, I decided to contribute to the menu and made my Italian Macaroni Salad (recipe on page 54) and my Rice Salad. The following week we attended the theatre. The Swamp Meadow Summer Children's Theatre presented "Scheherazade and the Arabian Nights."

What a simply delightful performance by these amazing kids, who ranged in age from the oldest at 15 to the youngest at 6 years old. It was our first time seeing a performance at the Swamp Meadow Theatre, but it will not be the last.

The following day we attended the Foster Better Barns and Garden Tour, a Foster Preservation Society sponsored event. This is a self-guided tour to some historic and unique barns and gardens in Foster. It was the first time that I attended the tour and unfortunately we were only able to visit three of the properties that day.

When Sal asked me to go to the first barn tour two years ago, I'm sorry to say, I declined. I mean, really, who wants to see barns? Now I'm sorry I missed it and I am looking forward to the next one.

Well, enough said about our boring two weeks in the country! Since moving to Scituate in 1993, our social schedule has been far from boring. We have met some wonderful people, made new friends, and attended some wonderful events.

So this month I am going to give you the rice salad recipe as I adapted from a recipe given to me by a friend. Her recipe used instant minute rice and have fewer ingredients.

Chicken Rice Salad

1 ½ cups uncooked Royal blend rice (white, brown, wild & red)
2 cups cubed cooked chicken breasts
1 cup frozen peas (thawed)
½ cup chopped celery
½ cup chopped dried apricots
½ cup cranraisins
½ cup raisins
½ toasted slivered almonds

Dressing

1 tablespoon white wine vinegar
3 tablespoon virgin olive oil
1 tablespoon lime juice
1 teaspoon minced fresh mint
½ teaspoon salt & pepper

Cook rice according to the package directions, cool. In large bowl combine the chicken, peas, celery, apricots, Cranraisins, raisins and almonds.

Combine oil, lime juice, mint, salt, and pepper- shake well. I grate the lime zest into the dressing; and use virgin olive oil and white balsamic vinegar.

When rice is cool, stir into chicken mixture, drizzle with the dressing and toss to coat. Chill for a least one-hour before serving. You can also use rice vinegar in place of the white vinegar. My advice is to use your imagination to spice up any recipe.

October 2008

October is a special month in our home; it is filled with both happy and sad memories. The bittersweet memories are the anniversary of the deaths of my maternal grandmother, Michelina Iantosco Bevelaqua and my father, Joseph Grossi. I think about my Grandmother every time I make one of her recipes and remember all the good times. I have my father to thank for my, shall we say, " fondness" for chocolate… naturally, he's often in my thoughts.

The happy occasions are Sal's birthday, our wedding anniversary, my sister AnneMarie's birthday, my niece Tanya's wedding anniversary and our annual trip to Hershey, Pennsylvania.

We have a sign that hangs in our rumpus room (how many of my readers out there know what a rumpus room is?) that states "Every October Hershey, the rest of the year is just waiting." For the antique car enthusiasts, the Hershey Car Show and Flea Market is like a grown up version of Disney World! Fans are in heaven, looking at old car parts, advertisements, gas pumps, gas station signs, and of course old cars. There are acres and acres of car parts, automobile related items and antique cars to look at and haggle over the price with the vendors and all while the smell of chocolate is in the air! It is truly an incredible event; there are hundreds of thousands of people from all over the world who attend this extravaganza.

As you walk around, looking at cars that have been restored to better than new condition, you hear many different languages spoken, and meet people from all walks of life who share a love for the antique automobile. We have been making this trek to Hershey every year since the early 1980's.

As my women readers can imagine, I wasn't particularly enthusiastic about going on a vacation to walk through fields and fields of old, rusty car parts. I mean like, really, does this sound like fun? So I said to Sal, "Let's make a deal. I'll go to Hershey if we go to Pennsylvania Dutch country too."

The first part of the week, we travel to the Amish area visiting little towns like "Bird-in-Hand," checking out the antique stores in the area, and shopping in all the local establishments. The rest of the week, we walk the fields, look at the cars, go out to dinner with friends, and on Friday night Sal sings in the talent show. He always gets called back to the stage to sing the Monster Mash, while I dressed as a witch complete with broom, dance in the background.

In the early days going to Hershey was more of an adventure then it is today. Back a few years ago most of the area surrounding Hershey Park was fields. Besides the flea market vendors and the car corral, they allowed campers to park right near all the action. For a daily fee, you were able to park the camper, with no hookup for water or electricity and to be able to put out your canopy.

We always arrived on Sunday and waited in line to get a good spot, right near Chocolate World (with indoor bathrooms) and the building with showers (where for $3.50 you received a mini bar of soap and the use of a towel). We loved this location, because it was right near the car corral and we could watch the antique cars arrive for the show on Saturday.

For years, we parked in this location and all our friends could find us and stop in for a visit and a meal. The show fields are all paved now and you're not allowed to park a camper close to the action anymore, so we now stay at a hotel. I really miss going in the camper and cooking for all our friends.

I always made gravy for macaroni & meatballs, lasagna, eggplant Parmesan, and dough for homemade pizza. I know I have already given my recipe for gravy (that's red-not brown) and for eggplant Parmesan and I will save the lasagna recipe for some other time.

I am going to give you my recipe for another staple I always brought to Hershey, chili. My high school friend, Karen Wilson, reminded me she had taught me to make chili, when I recently visited with her.

I am on the planning committee for my 40th reunion for Mt. Pleasant High School and I had been looking for Karen for the last ten years, having heard that she was in a nursing home recovering from an illness.

Karen became a successful model right out of high school and traveled all over the world. Another classmate Lauren and I visited her last week and while we were reminiscing, she reminded me of the time she taught me to make chili. Being an Italian girl, I had never tried chili before that time. I have since become more adventurous with trying new foods and flavors!

So here is my version of...

Above: *October 1995- The overview of the car show.*
Below: *October 1995- Me standing in front of a Cushman scooter at the Hershey Antique Car Show*

Karen's Famous Chili

2 tablespoons olive oil
2 medium onions, minced
1 red pepper, diced
6 cloves garlic, minced
¼ cup chili powder
1 tablespoon ground cumin
2 teaspoons ground coriander
1 teaspoon oregano (I omit the oregano as it can cause problems for some people)
1 teaspoon red pepper flakes
½ teaspoon cayenne pepper (or more to taste)

Fresh chili peppers, diced small to taste (can omit if you like a milder chili and it's hard to judge how hot the chili peppers are, so be careful. It's better to add, and harder to take away the heat!)
2 lbs. lean ground beef
2 (15 oz.) cans red kidney beans (I always used pinto beans that I have cooked myself since I like my beans firm, not mushy)
2 (28 oz.) cans of tomatoes (puree in blender) You can also use diced tomatoes and 1 can of tomato puree.

This recipe serves 6 to 8 people. Heat the oil in a large pan over medium heat until shimmering but not smoking. Add the onions, peppers, and all the spices, stirring often, until the vegetables are softened. Cooking the spices with the garlic and onions allows them to develop their flavors fully in the cooking oil.

Increase the heat to medium-high, and stir in the ground beef about 1 lb. at a time. You will need to break up any chunks with a wooden spoon and continue cooking until no longer pink. Stir in the tomatoes and beans and simmer over low heat until the beef is tender and the chili is dark, rich, and slightly thicken. I usually simmer the chili for about two hours. If is get too thick, add some water or wine and simmer some more. Serve with lime wedges, fresh diced tomatoes, diced avocado, sliced scallions, sour cream and/or shredded Monterey Jack cheese.

November 2008

Last month Sal and I participated in the 15th anniversary tour to Martha's Vineyard with our car club the Yankee Wood Chapter of the National Woody Club. Since

joining the club, we have made wonderful friends, who not only share a love for wood bodied antique cars, but also love to cook and entertain. Well we started to discuss the upcoming holidays and how our traditions have changed over the years.

September 2008 - On tour with the girls of the Yankee Wood chapter.

Many of us are Italian American and share similar memories and customs. We started to reminisce about Thanksgiving and what it was like for us growing up. Thanksgiving was an all-day affair, with my grandparents, my immediate family, and many aunts, uncles and cousins.

Since Thanksgiving was an all-American holiday, we had the traditional turkey dinner with all the trimmings. However, being Italian, we added a few more courses to the traditional dinner. The first course was always an antipasto platter, with prosciutto, capicola, salami, olives, provolone cheese, roasted peppers, anchovy fillets, and stuffed artichokes. Next came chicken escarole soup with mini veal meatballs (what is now called Italian wedding soup -- not that we ever called it that!), then we would have lasagna, with meatballs and sausage and finally the turkey dinner with all the trimmings. After the meal, there would be a variety of desserts, pies, cookies, fruit, roasted chestnuts, mixed nuts coffee and espresso.

By that time it was late afternoon and the men were watching football on TV (actually, they were sleeping in front of the TV) and the women were washing dishes. Later, in case anyone was still hungry, we would make sandwiches and eat leftovers. Growing up it never seemed like it was too much food, it was just normal.

It was wonderful sharing food and conversations with all the relatives. The relatives that had dinner elsewhere would always stop by to visit with my grandparents. It was a day of the never-ending meal! Anyway back to my discussion with my friends and the recipe I want to share with my readers, we talked about the different ways we stuff artichokes.

Here is my recipe for stuffed artichokes. This recipe serves 8.

Carciofi Ripieni "Stuffed Artichokes"

8 medium artichokes
¾ cup plain Italian bread crumbs
¼ cup chopped fresh parsley (flat-leaf variety)
¼ cup freshly grated Pecorino Romano & Parmigiano-Reggiano
2 garlic cloves, very finely chopped
4 thin slices of prosciutto (preferably Parma) finely chopped
Fresh ground pepper and about ¼ cup virgin olive oil

With a large knife, trim off the top 1-inch of the artichokes. Rinse them well under cold water. Cut off the stems so that the artichokes can stand upright. Peel off the tough outer skin of the stems and set aside. Bend back and snap off the small leaves around the base of each artichoke.

With scissors, trim the pointed tops off the remaining leaves. Remove the choke with a small knife with a rounded tip to scrape out the fuzzy leaves in the center. If you choose not to remove the choke before cooking, don't forget to remove it when you eating it. The heart of the artichoke is underneath the choke and worth all the work to get at it.

Finely chop the artichoke stems, mix with the breadcrumbs, parsley, cheese, prosciutto, and garlic and pepper to taste. Add a little olive oil and toss to moisten the stuffing evenly. Gently spread the leaves apart and lightly stuff the artichokes with the breadcrumb mixture.

Place the artichokes in a pot just wide enough to hold them upright. Add water to come to a depth of about ¾ inch around the artichokes. Drizzle the artichokes with the remaining olive oil, cover the pot and place over medium heat. When the water comes to a simmer, reduce the heat to low. Cook until the bottoms are tender when pierced and a leaf pulls out easily, about 45 minutes. Check occasionally and add warm water if necessary to prevent scorching. Serve warm or at room temperature.

To eat the artichoke, you pull out a leaf and scrape the bottom of the leaf and the stuffing with your teeth. When you get to the bottom of the choke, you have reached the heart and it is the very best part of the artichoke.

December 2008

November has come and gone and Christmas is just around the corner and it's time to start making the cookies. For as long as I can remember, my family has always made cookies. I can remember watching my grandmother and great grandmother, Antoinetta Iantosco, making cookies and being given some dough to play with to keep me quiet. That wasn't an easy job, as my grandmother would always call me a "chiaccherona" which means chatterbox in Italian.

Every Christmas, my grandmother, Michelina Bevelaqua made dozens and dozens of cookies to give as presents; there would be a tray for the mailman, the milk man, the soda man, cousins, friends and family. She always had homemade cookies in the house for when company came to visit. Grandma Bevelaqua knew all her recipes by heart, there was nothing written down, there were no measurements, it was all by rote. The amazing thing was that the cookies always came out just right. My grandmother died in 1985 at the age of 91 and she was still baking cookies well into her eighties.

My mother continues the same tradition and bakes cookies during the season. She always says that it just doesn't feel like Christmas unless she makes at least a few batches of cookies. I remember as a child, she would make chocolate chip, oatmeal, or molasses cookies for my sister, brother and I to have after school. She was always clipping out a new recipe to try. To this day, and she is 94 years young, my mother is still trying out new recipes.

Growing up, I think the only store brought cookie I ever ate was an Oreo®. I recall eating an Oreo® with my father. Of course I would separate the cookie and eat the crème filling first, just like he did, then dip the cookie in a glass of milk.

Italians not only make cookies at Christmas, we also make them for weddings and showers. I can still see my mother and my Aunt Lottie laughing as they were putting together the trays of cookies for my wedding.

My mother must have made "57 varieties" and they were trying to make sure each tray had the same number and same variety of cookie in each. Let me tell you it was not an easy feat to accomplish, but boy did the guests enjoy eating them!

Whenever I make Bourbon Balls, I remember the first time that I tried that recipe. It quickly became my father's favorite cookie. That Christmas he introduced Sal's nephew Frankie, who was about 10 years old at the time, to that particular cookie. Between the two of them, they ate all the Bourbon Balls out of all the trays of cookies that I made that year. It's still the first cookie Frankie looks for in the tray.

Baking at this time of year brings flashes of so many wonderful memories and observing the tradition keeps my grandmother and father alive in my heart.

So please try my recipes for prune filled Italian egg biscuits and Bourbon Balls and make your own memories.

July 1976 - My grandma, Michelina Iantosco Bevelaqua.

Prune Filled Italian Egg Biscuits

5 cups flour
5 teaspoons baking powder
1 cup sugar
¼ teaspoon salt
3 eggs
¾ cup milk
¾ cup oil
1 tablespoon anise extract (I use sambuca or anisette liqueur)

Sift flour, baking powder, sugar, and salt in a large bowl. Make a well in the center. Beat eggs and pour into the well. Add milk, oil and the liqueur. Mix well to form a blended dough. Place on a lightly floured board and knead lightly until dough is smooth. (You may have to add a little flour to keep from sticking).

Divide the dough into two or three pieces. Roll each out into a rectangle about ¼ inch thick. Spread filling down the center. Fold sides up over the filling and seal like a jellyroll. Place on a cookie sheet and bake at 375° until done, about 10 minutes. Cool. Mix ¼ cup lukewarm water with enough confectioners' sugar to make a thin glaze. Use to frost the cookies, shake colored sprinkles over the damp frosting.

To make as Egg Biscuits, break off pieces and roll to make snake like ropes 7 to 8 inches long and about the thickness of your thumb. Coil on a greased cookie sheet; the center should be slightly higher than the other edges. Bake in preheated 375° oven until done, but not brown, about 10 minutes. They should be pale tan in color. Cool then frost with glaze.

Prune Filling

Simmer a combination of chopped pitted prunes, apricots, dried pears about 2 lbs. in enough water to cover until tender. About 10 to 15 minutes, add about ½ square grated unsweetened chocolate to the mixture, 1 cup finely chopped walnuts, some chopped maraschino cherries and teaspoon of orange marmalade. Cook until the mixture is thickened. I also add about tablespoon of orange liqueur to the mixture.

Bourbon Balls

1 package (12oz) vanilla wafers, finely crushed
1 cup confectioners' sugar
1 cup finely chopped pecans
¼ cup light corn syrup
2 tablespoons unsweetened cocoa
½ cup bourbon
½ cup granulated sugar

In large bowl, mix thoroughly all ingredients, except the granulated sugar. Shape into 1" balls and then roll in sugar. Store in tightly covered container for at least two days before serving.

Left: *1954 - My mom standing in front of a fireplace at Aunt Lottie's house around Christmas time.* *Right:* *1980 - Me posing in my kitchen in Woonsocket.*

January 2009

Here I sit in front of my computer, thinking about all of the things I have yet to accomplish before Christmas Eve, which is just six days away, and wondering what in the world I'm going to write about for the January issue. Although Christmas is my favorite time of year, it is also the most stressful, with all the festivities, purchasing and wrapping gifts, decorating the house, and of course cooking.

December starts with a weekend away with our friends in our car club for the annual Yankee Wood Chapter Holiday Party. Each year we go to a different Bed and Breakfast or Inn in New England for the weekend. This year we traveled to the York Harbor Inn in York, Maine.

We always have a great time together, shopping, checking out the local antique stores, and having wonderful meals. We are truly blessed to have made such wonderful friends, who share a love for those wood bodied antique automobiles. We have a great time and I relax before I have to start my marathon cooking for our Christmas Party the next weekend, baking cookies to give away as gifts, and our open house on Christmas Eve.

This year I started cooking the week before our Maine trip as I decided to make candy to give to my friends as gifts. I made apricots that I poached and then dipped half in bittersweet chocolate and sprinkled with pistachio nuts, rosemary spiced roasted nuts, and candy bark.

I found these great containers at Job Lot, which looked like Chinese takeout, but in decorative colors. Since the candy bark was such a great hit with my friends, I decided I would make more to give to my staff for the holidays. So back I went to Job Lot for more containers, but alas there were no more to be found.

However, as I was picking up the multitudes of candy bars to make the bark, a woman remarked that someone must like chocolate. I explained to her that I was making candy bark to give away for gifts and that I would include the recipe for the next Mangia with Micheline. The original recipe was given to me by my friend and colleague, Terry Smith, who made the candy for her staff one Christmas. It was so good that her staff named it "Christmas Crack" because it was so addicting.

I am going to give you the original recipe, but I have many variations.

First, instead of saltine crackers, I use Keebler® Club Crackers. Second, I used a variety of different chocolates. For instance, I melt bittersweet chocolate (about 5 of the 3.5 oz. bars) with roasted hazelnuts, or white chocolate with crushed peppermint candy, semisweet with slivered almonds, espresso chocolate with pecans… the combinations are endless.

I melt the chocolate over a double boiler, rather than in the microwave, as there is better control over the melting process.

So here is the basic recipe, try it and experiment with the chocolate of your choice.

Candy Bark

Line large cookie sheet with foil and spray with Pam®

Cover with saltine crackers

Bring 2 sticks butter and ½ cup of sugar to a boil, stirring constantly for about for about 3 minutes, watch carefully as it will rise.

Pour over saltine crackers

Bake In 350° oven for approximately 7 to 8 minutes

Cover with Hershey® candy bars (about 6 bars), when melted spread over the cracker mixture.

Sprinkle with chopped nuts.

Let dry, break Into pieces

February 2009

It's been snowing for the last two days, and as I look out my window at the beautiful pristine white landscape I remembered our first winter in Scituate. Sal and I moved here in October of 1993. That winter, we had 22 snowstorms. I know, because I counted them! We were now in Salty's famous "No School Scituate-Foster-Glocester" Snow Belt! It's funny how we ended up in Scituate in 1993.

We were living in Providence in a wonderful Art Deco house, which was close by everything... work, stores, the freeway; but the neighborhood was changing. Still, we liked our house and we were really not looking to move just yet. However, one fateful day, we decided to take a ride and see where our friends, Debbie and Peter, had built their new home. While taking the grand tour of their home, I just happened to mention to Peter that when we were ready to move to the country, Scituate was one of the places I liked. I had fond memories of drives through the town with my parents.

My Uncle Frank and Aunt Helen Grossi moved to Scituate in the 1960's and my father would often take a ride up to the country to visit them. I remember my mother would ask my father to take a ride to the water, meaning the ocean, and my father would end up in Scituate. I guess my father thought the Reservoir had water even if it wasn't the ocean.

Anyway, those off the cuff remarks sent Peter on a mission. A few weeks later, he called us about a house next door to him that was for sale and would we like to see it. We decided to check it out, even though we really were not in the market to buy another house.

So Peter called the real estate agent and made an appointment for us to see the house. The three of us went to check it out. That house really wasn't my kind of house, but we thanked Peter and went on our way.

A few more weeks went by, and Peter called again. He said there was this great ranch house that he and Debbie had almost bought two years before, but the couple had taken it off the market before they could put a bid on it.

Well I told Peter, I wasn't interested that I just didn't like ranch style houses. Later that night, Debbie called and described the house to me, which she called an executive style ranch house. Let's just say that Debbie's description intrigued me enough to want to check it out.

So, once again Peter called the real estate agent and made the appointment for us to see the house the following Saturday. Peter also called his friends, David and Judy, who happened to live next door and asked them how many other people had already looked at the house. On that fateful Saturday morning, the three of us, Peter, Sal and I arrived to check out this house.

It is a wonderful house, well made, and designed for easy entertaining, with a great deal of character. We just fell in love with it. We were there about an hour, when we noticed another car pulling into the driveway. I asked the real estate agent who they were, and he said they were the next appointment to see the house. I looked at Sal and he looked at me, and I said that I didn't want them to see the house; that we wanted to buy the house.

He asked if we wanted to put in a bid and I said no, that we wanted to buy the house! That's how we bought our house in one hour, when we really weren't looking to buy a new home, and in fact ended up paying two mortgages for two years until we could sell our Providence property.

I knew it was our destiny, when we walked into the house. We both knew that this would be our home. Fate has been kind to us, we couldn't ask for better neighbors than David and Judy. We are members of a wonderful church family at Trinity and we have made so many friends in Scituate, Foster and Greene. That first winter, I really got a taste for what it was like to live in the Snow Belt of Rhode Island.

I thought I would share the recipe for one of the meals that I like to make in the winter. It is great with a salad and crusty Italian bread. It's a meal you can make for two or a crowd. The following is a recipe for four.

Christmas Eve 1993 - Peter and Deb Garafalo.

Clockwise from top: *June 1954 - My sister's high school prom with my dad, mom, sister AnneMarie, brother Joe and me. June 1954 - Me, my mom, and brother Joe sitting with Pretty Boy at our home on Borden Street. August 1954 - Visiting my Uncle John Riccetelli, who always had M&Ms, for my birthday, at his home on Union Street. February 1941 - Joe and Pete Bevelaqua chilling in the old neighborhood.*

Roasted Sausages, Peppers, Potatoes, Onions, and Carrots

1 lb. potatoes, peeled and cut into 1 inch chunks
1 each green, red, yellow bell peppers, cored, seeded and cut into 1 inch pieces
1 medium onion, cut into 1 inch chunks
1 lb. baby carrots
¼ cup olive oil
1 lb. Italian pork sausages, cut into 2" to 3" pieces
Couple cloves of garlic, crushed
Freshly ground pepper to taste

Preheat the oven to 450.° Spread the vegetables in a single layer in a large shallow roasting pan; do not crowd them, or they will not brown. Drizzle with the oil and sprinkle with pepper to taste. Stir well. Roast the vegetables, stirring once or twice, for about 45 minutes. Add the crushed garlic and stir. If using links of sausage, pierce each one in two or three places with a fork. Place the sausage on top of the vegetables. Bake for 15 to 30 minutes or until the sausages and vegetables are cooked through. Serve hot.

Note: I only use sausage from Graziano's, located on Charles Street in Providence. You can also get his sausage at the Oakland Deli in Cranston. It is very lean and not made in links. A close second is the sausage from Dave's market in Smithfield. Once you try a well-made sausage I guarantee you won't be able to eat the supermarket brands. There is a world of difference in flavor, texture and grease!

March 2009

Once again I'm at my computer writing this month's column and I wondered how the month of March came to be named. So I decided to look up the meaning on Wikipedia.com and here is what I found. "March, the third month of the year in the Gregorian Calendar, and is one of the seven months, which are 31 days long.

The name of March comes from ancient Rome, when March was the first month of the year and named Martius after Mars, the Roman god of war. It is also the month that Christians celebrate St. Patrick's (17th) and St. Joseph's (19th) Days.

When I think of March, I think of corned beef, Irish bread, doughboys and zeppoli.

Sal and I like to attend church suppers, not only for the wonderful food, but also for the opportunity to make new acquaintances.

Of course, the main meal in March is corned beef and cabbage. When we first joined Trinity Church, I joked with John Del Selva, who was attempting to sell me tickets, that is just wasn't fair to forget about St. Joseph's Day. So, I made a deal that the Lombardi's would donate the zeppoli for dessert.

Earlier this week, I drove over to La Salle Bakery in Providence and ordered 15 dozen zeppoli for the Saturday, March 21st Trinity Church St. Patrick - St. Joseph Day supper. My high school friends, Cheryl and Mike Manni, own La Salle Bakery and always are so generous when I buy the zeppoli for the church. They also make great pastry!

The first corned beef and cabbage dinner we are scheduled to attend is at the Greene Public Library on March 7th and I promised to make some Irish bread for that supper. Since I have already shared my recipes for the Irish bread and doughboys, I figured it was time for the zeppoli recipe. I clipped this recipe out of the Providence Journal about 25 years ago. zeppoli are golden brown puffed pastry (Sfingi-cream puff), filled with sweet yellow cream and topped with a red cherry.

Sfingi Di San Giuseppe "Zeppoli"

½ cup butter
1 ¼ cup flour
1 cup water
2 Eggs

Beat eggs well. Bring water and butter to a boiling point. When all the butter is melted, turn down the heat and gradually add flour, stirring well. When almost cool, add egg mixture a little at a time and mix thoroughly. Drop by tablespoon onto a greased cooking sheet. Bake in 425° oven for 20 minutes. Cool, cut in half, and fill with the yellow cream, pipe some cream around the top and place the cherry on top.

1983 - Sal & Miki ready for the Easter parade in Providence.

Cream Napoletana

8 tablespoons sugar
6 egg yolks
6 tablespoons flour
1-quart milk
Vanilla, lemon or rum flavor

Beat sugar and egg yolks until creamy; blend in flour. Slowly add milk and stir well. Pour into a double boiler and desired favoring (vanilla, lemon, or rum). Stir constantly with a wooden spoon until thick. Whip with eggbeater until glossy. Remove from heat. When cool, fill the zeppoli.

April 2009

It's April, so it must be spring! Although, considering I am writing this on the first official day of spring, it's not that warm out today. However the sun is shining, it's a Friday and a payday to boot, so all in all, it is a good day. I've been going through my many recipes looking for some ideas for hors d'oeurves to share with my readers this month.

Actually, I have another reason to go into the many different locations (kitchen, breakfast room, bedroom, dining room, and cellar to name a few places) to hunt down just the right recipe to share.

About two years ago, I was looking for something to do in my spare time. I have always been involved in various community service agencies in a volunteer capacity. After being the President of the Board of Directors of the YWCA of Greater RI for about 10 years, as well as being both an Executive Board member and the President of my Union, I decided I needed a rest.

After a few years, I must admit that I became bored and I was looking for new challenges. Then one day, I met Bill Vangel and just happen to ask him about The Scituate Rotary Club and as the saying goes - the rest is history! I have met some wonderful people in our Rotary Club and learned of many community service projects that The Rotary does all around the world. I've spread mulch around at the playground, discovered that giving blood is not my thing, sung carols at the Nancy Ann Nursing Home, attended "Million Dollar Meals" and made good friends.

Now I am helping to prepare the food for our first ever wine tasting, being held on April 18th at the beautifully restored Edgewood Manor. So, if you like wine, good food, making friends, having fun and fellowship, check out our ad in this wonderful publication. I have two recipes that I found while searching in my archives that I would like to share with you this month. The first is a hot hors d'oeurves and the second is a hot dip.

2000 - Linda Cipriano at our birthday bash
where we turned a half a century old in the new century.

Hot Sausage and Cheese Puffs

1 lb. of hot or sweet sausage
1 lb. sharp cheddar cheese, shredded
Diced yellow, red, orange, green peppers (about ½ pepper each color)
3 cups Bisquick® baking mix
¾ cup water (I used white wine instead)

Remove sausage from casings and cook in a large skillet, breaking up the meat with a fork, for about 10 minutes. Drain off all the fat, spoon sausage into a large bowl and cool completely.

Crumble the sausage with a fork, and add the shredded cheese, Bisquick® mix, diced peppers and water. Mix until all is well blended. Roll into 1" balls and place about 2: apart from each other on cookies sheet.

Bake in a 400° oven for 12 to 15 minutes or until puffed and browned. Cool and serve. This can be frozen. To serve after freezing, reheat in 375° oven for 10 to 12 minutes.

Buffalo Chicken Wing Dip

3 cups cooked shredded chicken
⅔ cup hot sauce
2 8 oz. packages cream cheese
⅓ cup blue cheese dressing
1 cup cheddar cheese
½ cup crumbled blue cheese

Soften cream cheese, add hot sauce, blue cheese dressing and ½ cup cheddar cheese. When mixed, add all of the chicken and mix well. Spread into a baking dish, top with the remaining cheese and bake at 350° for 30 minutes. Serve with chips.

May 2009

It's funny how time flies as we get older. It seems like just yesterday we were complaining about the long cold snowy winter and now it's May. It's time to get out the 1941 Cadillac and drive to the first show of the season in Rhinebeck, New York. April was a busy month for me, with Easter and of course the first annual Scituate Rotary Wine Tasting.

It was a wonderful event. Everyone who attended enjoyed good food, wonderful wines and a chance to bid on some great items graciously donated by our area merchants. The monies raised will be used by the Scituate Rotary to give back to the community.

If any of my readers are looking to get involved in a wonderful organization, where there is fun, fellowship and a purpose in service to others, check us out some Wednesday night at Chester's Restaurant, where we meet at 7:00 pm for a dinner meeting.

This month I am hosting another Pot-Luck Dinner for my high school reunion committee. The Mt. Pleasant High School class of 1968 has really come together after the reunion, friends that haven't seen each other in 40 years are now back in each other's lives and we have vowed not to become strangers again.

Anyway, I am once again going through my recipes looking for something different to make. I came across a recipe given to me by a friend. It is simple to make and very tasty, so I thought I would share it with you. It can be made for dinner for two or for a dinner party for many, just adjust the ingredients accordingly.

Chicken Cutlet Casserole

Olive Oil
2 lbs. chicken cutlets
1 cup bread crumbs, seasoned with garlic, basil, pepper and oregano
¼ cup Romano cheese
2 tablespoons soften butter
1 small jar marinated artichoke hearts, drained
1 8oz. jar roasted red peppers, drained
8 oz. pepper jack cheese, shredded

Coat bottom of a 13" x 9" casserole dish with olive oil. Place uncooked chicken in a single layer. Mix breadcrumbs (seasoned with garlic, basil, pepper, and oregano) with butter and Romano cheese. Spread over chicken.

Cut artichokes and roasted peppers into small pieces. Arrange over the crumb mixture. Top with Pepper Jack Cheese. Bake uncovered for 1 hour in a 350°oven.

Our 1941 Cadillac 60 special

June 2009

Have you ever thought about the connections we make in life? Sometimes we meet someone and that person has a profound effect on your life. It can be a teacher, who made learning fun. It can be a co-worker that helps you learn a new job.

Connections are like circles, overlapping through time, circles that connect one person to another. You can become friends with your friend's friends and your circle grows. I have discovered through my life's work that how I treat the people I deal with can change their life.

There have been former probationers that search me out just to tell me how well they are doing now. I have found that you never know what effect you can have on another human being, just by treating them with respect, really listening, and giving praise when a goal is accomplished. Sometimes a random act of kindness can have a ripple effect.

Last year, I co-chaired the 40th High School Reunion for the Mount Pleasant Class of 1968. We had a truly great committee that worked together and planned a wonderful event. In the process of planning this event, a remarkable thing happened, connections that were there in high school, but were lost, are back. We have rediscovered friendships and made new friends.

This core group of classmates is having breakfast every other month, we are busy planning a summer event and next year we are planning a 60th birthday bash. Last month, I hosted a potluck dinner for my classmates, it was an excuse to get together to reminisce about high school and brainstorm ideas for future activities. That of course started me thinking about connections.

Anyway, I was looking for a new dish to make for the potluck. I found a recipe on the Internet on the food and wine site that sounded like it would be ok with some adjustments. Everyone at the potluck liked the dish, I hope you will too.

Baked Rigatoni with Sausage, Spinach, Ricotta, and Fontina

1 lb. rigatoni
1 lb. hot Italian sausage
3 tablespoons virgin olive oil
1 10 oz. package fresh spinach, chopped
2 cups (about 1 lb.) part-skim ricotta cheese
5 tablespoons grated Parmesan cheese
½ teaspoon grated nutmeg
¼ teaspoon fresh-ground black pepper
¼ teaspoon salt
6 oz. Fontina cheese, grated (about 1 ½ cups)

Heat the oven to 450° Oil a 9-by-13-inch baking dish. Remove the sausage from the casing and cook, chopping the meat into small pieces.

In a large pot of boiling, salted water, cook the rigatoni until almost done, about 12 minutes. Drain. Put the pasta in the prepared baking dish and toss with 1 tablespoon of the oil.

Meanwhile, put the spinach in a food processor and chop, then mix with the ricotta, sausage meat, 3 tablespoons of the Parmesan, the nutmeg, salt, and pepper. Stir in half the fontina. Stir the spinach mixture into the pasta. Top with the remaining fontina and Parmesan. Drizzle the remaining 2 tablespoons oil over the top. Bake the pasta until the top is golden brown, 15 to 20 minutes.

<u>**Note:**</u> *The original recipe did not have sausage and called for frozen spinach and whole milk ricotta cheese. I always use fresh spinach and I do not cook it prior to adding to the dish. Spinach cooks fast and will water out. Frozen spinach has to be firmly squeezed to remove all of the water .*

July 2009

Can you believe it is July already? It seems like just yesterday there was snow on the ground and we couldn't wait for the summer. July is jam packed with activities. The night before the Fourth there is chowder & clam cakes at the Hope-Jackson Fire Station and the Old Time Fiddlers on the North Scituate Green.

July 4th is Scituate's Old Home Days. Sal, who has been dubbed "the Checker Master," will be returning to play checkers with the kids. The Scituate Rotary is holding its second annual Fourth of July breakfast (real bargain at five dollars a ticket) at the Community House, so I'll be busy "working the dining room."

The following weekend, we are driving the '41 Cadillac up to Castle in the Clouds and Castle Springs in New Hampshire for an Antique Car Show. This "castle," built at the turn of the century in the arts & crafts style, sits way up on top of a hill with spectacular views of the surrounding area. We will be meeting some of our friends from our car club, so it will be fun.

The last weekend in July a quaint country fair called "Foster Old Home Days" takes place, complete with its own Foster Idol Show. Last year, Sal made it to the Finals singing "Monster Mash". On Sunday, July 26, it's the Greene Public Library 17th Annual Chicken BBQ held at 818 Hopkins Hollow Road in Greene. That's another great bargain at ten dollars for adults and five dollars for children or better still twenty-five for a family of four.

I will be making my macaroni salad, the chicken & rice salad, and an Italian potato salad as a donation for the library. So come on down to Greene and sample some of my recipes. Where else but in rural America can you find interesting things to do, eat wonderful food and all at a bargain price! I thought I would share my recipe for Italian potato salad for this month's recipe. All ingredients are to taste and you need to adjust the amount for the quantity you need. The following should be just right for six people.

Micheline's Italian Potato Salad

4 to 6 medium Yukon Gold and/or Red Bliss Potatoes
2 stalks celery, sliced
1 medium red onion, chopped
Black and/or green olives, sliced
Red/yellow/orange pepper chopped (whatever color combination you like)
2 tablespoons capers, rinsed and drained (optional)
Fresh dill to taste
Salt/pepper to taste
Approximately ½ cup virgin olive oil
Approximately 3 to 4 tablespoons white balsamic/wine vinegar.

Put the potatoes in a medium saucepan with cold water to cover and add salt to taste. Cover and bring to a simmer over medium heat and cook until the potatoes are tender when pierced with a fork. (About 20 minutes)

You can either cook the potatoes whole, and when cool peel and cut into cubes or you can cut the potatoes beforehand and cook. I usually just wash the potatoes, cut them into cubes and not peel them as I like the skins on my potatoes. I have also used a combination of white, red, yellow and even purple potatoes.

Drain the potatoes, place in large bowl and add the other ingredients and then add the vinegar and oil while the potatoes are warm. Add the dill last. You can either serve the salad at room temperature or cold.

Remember you can experiment by adding whatever ingredients you like. Sometimes I just make it simple with potatoes, onions, celery, and olives. I have used red or white wine vinegar or tarragon vinegar. If I don't have dill I will use parsley or basil. Another variation of this salad uses fresh cooked green beans, red onion, and capers without the peppers and olives. Always add the spices to your taste.

August 2009

August is the last month of summer (if you can call the weather we been having so far a summer) and my birthday month. It's going to be a busy month, with attending the wedding of one of my staff members, a retirement party for my sister-in-law, and a cookout with my Mt. Pleasant High School classmates and that's just the first weekend.

Then it's off to an old fashioned Italian church feast in Connecticut, a visit with friends on Long Island and celebrating with several friends, who share birthdays this month. Last month, Sal and I drove to Wolfeboro, New Hampshire in the 1941 Cadillac to a car show at the Castle in the Clouds. We lucked out and actually had a warm and mostly sunny weekend, which is always a good thing when you are in an antique car. For those of you who remember vacuum wipers, need I say more?

We stayed at The 1810 House, a charming B&B, along with our friends, David & Doreen Salzman, later meeting up with Brian & Annette Burke for dinner at the 51 Mill Street Restaurant. Wolfeboro is a delightful town with a wonderful World War II museum, a wooden boat museum, and great views of Lake Winnipesaukee... well worth a visit.

However, I was disappointed that one of my favorite meals was not offered in the restaurant, so I thought I would find the recipe and share it with my readers. This is great served with Risotto or garlic mashed potatoes. This recipe serves 6.

Sal when he ran for office.- Photo by Hutnak Studios

Veal Osso Buco

2 tablespoons extra-virgin olive oil
6 2-inch-thick meaty veal shanks, each tied with string (¾ to 1 lb. each)
Salt and freshly ground pepper
2 large carrots cut into ½ -inch dice
1 medium onion cut into ½ -inch dice
1 celery rib cut into ½ -inch dice
2 garlic cloves, minced
1 cup dry red wine, such as Chianti
1 cup drained canned Italian tomatoes, coarsely chopped
1 cup chicken stock or canned low-sodium broth

Preheat the oven to 325°. Heat the olive oil in a large enameled cast-iron casserole dish. Season the veal shanks with salt and pepper and cook over moderate heat until browned, about 8 minutes per side. Transfer the shanks to a plate.

Add the carrots, onion, celery and garlic to the casserole. Reduce the heat to moderately low and cook, stirring, until tender, about 7 minutes. Add the wine and cook, scraping up any browned bits, until slightly reduced, about 5 minutes. Add the tomatoes and chicken stock and bring to a simmer over high heat.

Return the shanks to the casserole, nestling them into the vegetables; add any accumulated juices. Cover the casserole and braise the shanks in the oven for 1 hour. Turn the shanks, cover and cook for about 1 hour longer, until the meat is very tender. Transfer the shanks to a rimmed platter and cover loosely with foil. Measure the sauce; you should have 2 cups. If necessary, reduce the sauce over high heat. Season with salt and pepper.

Cut the strings off the shanks. Spoon the sauce on top and serve.

September 2009

Every time I get ready to write my column, I sit and think about what recipe to share. Next, I have to decide on what story to tell this month and somehow relate the story to the recipe. At first, I was going to tell you about visiting with our friends, David & Doreen at their home in Long Island, and the trips to the wineries.

I had planned to give you the recipe for a dish that Doreen and I made for her father-in-law, a healthier version of clams, shrimp and linguine. However, that recipe will have to wait, because I want to try to spice it up; and give it the Micheline twist before I share it.

I just didn't have enough time to experiment. Then, my focus changed after attending last night's Rotary meeting. The meeting had some very special guest speakers: four young men and two young women, students going into their senior year of high school.

Last May, they attended RYLA (Rotary Youth Leadership Awards) intensive leadership training program. They spoke at our club, because we had sponsored some of the participants. The four young men, spoke from their hearts and told us how this weekend changed their lives and their perspectives on leadership. They bonded with each other, and they became family.

The two young women spoke about the leadership skills they learned. Most importantly, the women learned that being a leader is not about being the boss. It is about leading your team to use their strengths to accomplish the task. With the exception of one young woman, who lives in Hope, all the others live in Massachusetts and attend the Massachusetts Regional Vocational School.

Their guidance teacher accompanied them to the meeting. She talked about how the students came back from that weekend with so many wonderful ideas. They

Me pictured here with the Moldova delegation and A.G. Patrick Lynch

have developed a mentoring program for the incoming freshmen class. In addition, all of the students are going back to RYLA as group leaders.

It was truly inspiring to listen to the voices of our future. Then the meeting turned to our upcoming visit by a delegation of high level Russian officials from Moldova, formally Romania in the Soviet Republic.

The Theme of The Open World Program is "Informing the Public about Combating Corruption." I will be arranging visits at District Court, the ACI and the Board of Elections, to name a few. Our visitors will be staying with Rotary Host Families and will learn firsthand about American Culture. I am very excited about this new opportunity for me to plan their visit. Therefore, I suppose you are wondering what recipe could possibly go hand in hand with this month's story. What else but a recipe for Russian Tea Cakes!

Chocolate Snowballs
A moist chocolate version of the popular Russian tea cakes

¾ cup unsalted cream butter	1 egg
¼ cup milk	½ teaspoon salt
¾ cup packed brown sugar	1 teaspoon vanilla
2 cups flour	¼ teaspoon baking soda
3 oz. unsweetened chocolate, melted	1 cup chopped nuts (pecans or walnuts)
1 teaspoon baking powder	confectioners' sugar

Preheat Oven 350°. Yield 5 dozen cookies (1 inch).
In a 3 quart mixing bowl, combine butter and brown sugar, beat at medium speed until light and fluffy. Add melted chocolate, egg, vanilla, milk and nuts; mix well. Sift together the dry ingredients (except confectioners' sugar) and add to mixture; blend well.

Chill 1 hour or until firm enough to shape into 1-inch balls, using a rounded teaspoon for each. Place about 2 inches apart on ungreased baking sheet. Bake near center of oven for 8 to 10 minutes.(8 minutes for a fudgier cookie; tops will still be soft).

Remove carefully from cookie sheet; roll immediately in confectioners' sugar to coat thoroughly. Cool on wire racks; roll again in sugar.

NOTE: *I mix cocoa with the confectioner's sugar for that added chocolate flavor.*

October 2009

October is a beautiful month, with its cool crisp air and all the trees wearing their fall colors. It is the last month before the temperature drops, the trees bare their branches, and we drag out those winter coats.

October's landscape is beautiful with all the colors; it is a joy to just take a ride and enjoy God's ever changing painting. Do you remember when we were kids and the big thing to do on Sunday was to take a drive? Our family would get into the car, my mother would have baked a cake or cookies and off we would go to visit family or friends. It was inexpensive entertainment. Memories were made each week.

Our parents grew up in the Depression and were not wealthy so, going out to a restaurant for dinner was rare and only for important occasions. People visited one another to play games and cards or went bowling for entertainment.

Sal and I like to go out to dinner every week. It is a treat because I do not have to cook it, serve it, or clean up after it. Yes, a real treat! The down side is that it can be expensive, the food mediocre and you wonder why you even bothered. I keep thinking I should start a dinner club with a few of my friends. Each couple would take turns having dinner at their home during the month. Since I'm such a control freak (I have mentioned that before), I would want to cook the whole meal from soup to nuts.

However, one way to defray the cost would be for someone to bring an appetizer, another a side dish and someone else the dessert. The couple hosting the party would make the main dish. After the meal, we could break out the cards and play games like crazy 8's, hi-low jack, or Trivial Pursuit. Maybe we just have to start thinking about some old-fashioned fun and low cost meals.

So here is a dish that does not cost a lot to make, is easy to prepare, and is delicious. I checked out this dish in a few of my numerous cookbooks (I check out the recipes, look for ideas and rarely follow the book) and was surprised that all the recipes were very different. None came close to how I make it.

This recipe translates to "hunter's style." Traditionally it is made with a whole chicken cut-up into pieces; I usually make it with chicken breasts. This recipe will serve four people. Serve with rice or a side of macaroni.

Chicken Cacciatore

1 lb. boneless chicken breast
1 onion, chopped
1 red pepper, chopped
1 large carrot, sliced thin
2 or 3 cloves garlic, crushed
Mushrooms (Portobello, white, porcini) sliced
A few sun dried tomatoes sliced into thin slivers
1 (28 oz.) can diced tomatoes w/juice
White or red wine, about a quarter cup
Basil, parsley, red pepper to taste
Virgin olive oil
Flour to dredge the chicken

Dredge the chicken pieces in flour to coat lightly, shake off the excess. In large sauté pan, heat oil over a medium high heat, brown the chicken on both sides and remove.

Add a little more oil if needed and cook the garlic, onions, carrot, peppers, sun dried tomatoes until onions are translucent, and mushrooms and vegetables are tender. Add wine and simmer until wine is

Halloween - Waiting for the Halloween parade on Danielson Pike in Scituate.

reduced by half. Add the tomatoes with its juice, parsley, red pepper, basil and simmer for a few minutes, add chicken back in the pan, turn to coat and cook until chicken is tender and cooked through.

Once chicken is done, remove and plate. If necessary, boil the sauce until it thickens slightly. Spoon sauce over the chicken, sprinkle with fresh basil and serve. Since this is hunter style, you can really add anything.

Sometimes I will add black olives, capers, or peas. If I use dried porcini mushrooms, I add the water from the mushrooms used to reconstitute the mushrooms to the sauce.

November 2009

I love October because it's the birth month of so many of the special people in my life. Sal and I were also married in October; this year was our 30th anniversary. It is also filled with bittersweet memories because it is the month my grandmother, father and now Uncle Tony died.

Last month I attended a memorial service for one of my best friends from high school. It was held on what would have been her 59th birthday. Karen Wilson and I were an "odd duo" and unlikely friends in the 60's. Karen was a tall classy beautiful black woman; I was a petite, Italian white woman. What made us the best of friends was the fact that we shared the same values; a love of family, a close relationship with our beloved grandmothers and a love of cooking. She was a very special woman, who lived life to the fullest, traveled the world as a first class model, but never forgot that family and friends were the most important part of life. I will miss her.

Dr. Anthony Lombardi, Sr., Uncle Tony, became my uncle from the first moment that Sal introduced us. Uncle Tony was the happiest when surrounded by his family and friends. He and I shared a love of cooking and I would often bring him a special bottle of olive oil or aged vinegar. I loved to listen to Uncle Tony and Sal talk about growing up on Federal Hill and sharing the family stories. He was a great educator and what a tribute it was to see so many of past and present students paying their respects. He touched so many lives, and will be missed.

So, in memory of my grandmother, father, uncle and friend, I am sharing one of my father's favorite cookies. The first time I made them, my father was eating them as fast as I baked them. So bake some cookies to share with that special relative or friend and make a memory to last a lifetime.

February 1954 - Sal's uncle, Anthony Lombardi
with Sal and his sister Anna.

Mincemeat Foldovers

Dough:
2 cups flour
¼ cup sugar
¼ teaspoon salt
8 oz. Cream cheese
1 cup butter

Filling:
1 cup mincemeat (may need more, I always do)

Glaze:
In small bowl mix glaze ingredients listed below until smooth
1 cup confectioners' sugar
2 tablespoons rum
2 teaspoons light corn syrup

350° oven 12-15 minutes. In a large bowl mix flour, sugar, & salt; using pastry blender or 2 knifes used scissors fashion, cut in the cream cheese & butter until mixture resembles cornmeal.

With your hands work dough until it holds together. Divide into 4 balls, wrap each in wax paper and refrigerator until dough is firm. Remove one section of dough to work at a time.

On lightly floured surface, roll into a 10" circle. With a 3" round cookie cutter, cut into circles. Place ½ teaspoon mincemeat into the center of the circle, and fold over the filling, seal the edges by pressing with a fork dipped in flour. Place on cookie sheet. Repeat with remaining dough, re rolling the scraps.

Bake about 12 to 15 minutes or until golden brown. (Depends on how thick you roll the dough). Remove to wire rack to cool, and drizzle with rum glaze. Makes about 4 dozen cookies.

December 2009

Did you ever have one of those eureka moments? You know that moment when it suddenly dawns on you that it has finally happened! I was reminded of one of my eureka moments as I was wandering around the booths at the Scituate Art Festival. I came across a booth that sold kitchen towels. There it was; a towel that said, "Mirror, Mirror on the wall, I am my mother after all."

Growing up, you never think that you are going to turn into your parents. You just know that you'll never be like them! Then all of a sudden, you are them. I vividly remember the very first time I realized that I was my mother. I had moved out of my parents' home into my first apartment (which was a feat in itself because Italian women do not move out of the house until they are married, or they are "fallen women") and it was Christmas time. I decided to make cookies to give away as gifts, following the Bevelaqua family tradition.

So I gathered all my recipes, took out all of my ingredients, set up my mixer, and set about making my Christmas cookies. Sal came over and decided he was going to help me bake by giving me advice on how to make the cookies. All of a sudden, I flashed on my mother and father having the same kind of discussion at the kitchen table. My father always liked his cookies to be on the large size and my mother made them small. It was at that moment that I realized that I was my mother after all!

Here are two cookie recipes that my mother always made for Christmas.

October 1979 - An argument over cigars at our wedding.

Date Nut Bars

Sift together:
1 cup sifted flour; 1 teaspoon baking powder; and 1 teaspoon salt.

Add: 1 ½ cups chopped dates; 1 cup chopped nuts (pecans or walnuts), Set Aside

Beat: 3 eggs until foamy

Add gradually: 1 cup packed brown sugar; beat well while adding.

Add: 1 teaspoon vanilla.
Fold in dry ingredients, dates and nuts. Beat well

Spread: evenly in a well-greased cookies sheet or 13"x 9" pan

Bake: 350° oven for 20-25 minutes until golden
Cut into bars while still warm and roll in sifted Confectioners' Sugar.

Thumbprint Cookies

Prepare: 1 ½ cups finely chopped nuts. Set aside

Mix thoroughly: ½ cup shortening; ½ cup soft butter; ½ cup packed brown sugar; 2 egg yolks; and 1 teaspoon vanilla.

Sifted together and stir in: 1 cup sifted flour and ½ teaspoon salt. Roll into balls the size of a walnut.

Beat slightly: 2 egg whites; Dip balls into egg whites; then roll in nuts. Place about 1" apart on greased baking sheet. Bake 5 minutes in 375° oven; remove from oven and press thumb gently in top of cookie.

Return to oven; bake 5 more minutes. When cool fill indentation with jelly or icing.

(Hint: I use a thimble to make the indentation.)

January 2010

Although you are reading this article in January, I am writing it in December right at deadline. Carol has suggested that I rename the column to "Midnight Mangia" since I am always writing after midnight. What can I say; I'm just a night person. I take after my mother, who at 95 stills bakes late at night. I'm hoping that I can beat the snow storm tomorrow to shop for a new stand mixer for her, since hers died the other day and she is in the middle of trying a new cookie recipe.

I am sharing a new brownie recipe with you this month. Sal and I always go to Christmas in the Valley, an arts & crafts fair sponsored by FosteringArts.org held each year in November. It is a wonderful time, with entertainment, beautiful handcrafted items, and unique items that make great gifts. We always buy wonderful soaps and lotions from Glocester Greens & Goats as well as handcrafted items for gifts.

The last few years, I always buy the gourmet herb, fruit & spice vinegars made by Thyme Farm Vinegars. Not only are the vinegars tasty, but Holly and Charlie Shadoian have the recipes, supplied free, for each of the flavored vinegars. They also make Charlie's Chili Stuff. They presented me with a challenge: could I make a dessert using the Chili mixture?

Well I thought about what would complement the hot chili spice and, of course, came up with my all-time favorite taste: chocolate. (Lindt makes a dark chocolate chili candy bar, which I have tried) I decided to make a brownie with a hint of cinnamon and the bite of hot spice. The brownie is not spicy, but has an after taste of heat. So here is the recipe, taste tested last night, the first time in print anywhere, right here in the fabulous *Foster Home Journal, Scituate Star & Glocester Gazette.*

Micheline's Mexicali Brownies

1 cup oil
⅔ cups cocoa
2 cups sugar
½ teaspoon baking powder
2 teaspoons vanilla
½ teaspoon salt
4 eggs
1 teaspoon cinnamon
1 cup flour
1 tablespoon Charlie's Chili Stuff

Blend oil, sugar and vanilla in a bowl. Add eggs, one at a time, beating well with a spoon. Combine flour, cocoa, baking powder, salt, cinnamon, and Charlie's chili stuff. Gradually add dry ingredients to the mixture, beat well to incorporate all ingredients. Spread in greased 15 x 10-inch pan. Bake at 350° for 15-20 minutes or until brownie puls away from the pan. Cool before cutting.

Note: You can order Charlie's Chili Stuff from Thyme Farm Vinegars, Foster, RI. (401) 397-2389 or use your own chili spice mixture.

Add your own twist...

February 2010

On January 15th, my mother, Mary Grossi, turned 96 years young. To celebrate this momentous occasion the family gathered at my brother Joe's house in Westerly for food, fun and memories. On the drive back, my mother and her youngest sister, Tessie, were reminiscing about growing up in Providence, working at the various factories, the hurricane of 1937, and how their brothers would play pranks on the relatives.

One story is that my uncles Pete and Joe would visit my Great Aunt Fanny and "borrow" her very nice Christmas ornaments right off her tree to decorate their tree. When Uncle Mike and Aunt Fanny came to visit, she would always comment that she had the same ornaments on her tree. I'm not quite sure that Aunt Fanny ever figured out that the ornaments traveled from her tree to theirs every year. Aunt Fanny lived to be 98 years old and she was a trip!

From left.: cousins Netta Iantosco DiSanto, Etta Iantosco Braun, Joan Iantosco D'Ambrosia, sister Tessie and Mom.

My mother is the oldest of eight, four boys and four girls. There is twenty years between my mother and my aunt Tessie. Neither my mother nor my aunt look their respective ages, in fact, my cousin Elaina quipped that day that she hopes that she inherited the Bevelaqua women's genes.

We discovered during that ride home that my aunt and Sal's mother, Anna Loffredo Lombardi (age 85), worked in the same factories around the same times. Our families grew up during the great depression and that experience colored the way they lived their lives. When they were old enough, they went to work to help support the family. They made do with what little they had, and had a way to stretch a meal to serve anyone who came to the table.

I have been privileged to grow up learning the ways to stretch a meal. Believe me it comes in handy, when Sal calls me up at the last minute and tells me he is bringing guests home for dinner and I have "nothing" in the house to cook. So this month I decided to share what I call one of my mother's depression dishes. I have added some ingredients to make it a hardy meal.

Patata Zuppa "Potato Soup"

Diced potatoes (amount depends on how many people you are serving) into small pieces (I like to use both Yukon Gold and red.)

Fry them in virgin olive oil for just about five minutes; add a couple of cloves of crushed garlic and cook until the garlic is golden. Then, carefully add water to the pan, enough to more than cover them, add lots of black pepper, some parsley and cook until potatoes are soft.

Meanwhile in a separate pan steam some escarole or Swiss chard, which has been cut up into bite size pieces. Once the potatoes are cooked, I will crush some of them or I will add a small amount of instant potatoes to thicken the soup. Then add the greens to the soup, add more water if necessary.

Last, but not least, I add one can (drained and rinsed) of chick peas. You can also use any other kind of bean instead, or spinach instead of the escarole or Swiss chard. Taste and adjust seasonings, add a little of virgin olive oil over the top and serve with a crusty Italian loaf of bread.

Simon, my great grand nephew, cooking Kayleigh Bledsoe, my great grand niece.

March 2010

For the past several weeks I have been on a mission to find a recipe for this month's article. I wanted a traditional Italian Easter recipe, but I had already shared the ones that I make every year. There I was discussing my dilemma with my manicurist, Ann-Marie Capaldi, (who is really more of a family member since she has been doing my nails for the last 23 years) when she mentioned the bread that her grandmother always made at Easter. She in turns calls her father, who tells me about the sweet bread that has Easter eggs baked in it, with the candy on the top.

Well since this was not a specialty of my family, I was on a search for a recipe. I found the recipe, but the question was still there about the eggs baked in the bread. Did you first boil the eggs and color them, then bake them? Did you place them in the bread uncolored raw and they would cook while the bread baked? Did you eat them after the bread was made? Or were they just decorations?

I asked my mother, who told me that my grandmother made the bread and the eggs were raw and not colored and cooked while they baked. She never did answer me about what to do with the eggs, but hey, the woman is 96 so she is forgiven for not telling me.

My hairdresser, Marie Penta, who was cutting my mother's hair when I asked the question, said that her grandmother made the bread and the eggs were colored and that they always ate the eggs.

I asked my friend, Laura Queenan, who remembers that her grandmother made the bread, and always let the dough rise on the television (TV's had tubes back then that gave off heat), covered with a towel, and heaven forbid if you made any movement that would "make the dough fall or you would be in big trouble." The egg question was still unanswered.

I asked Tina Gervasio Vangel, who said that, her grandmother made the bread with colored eggs and no one ate the eggs. Marie Zammarelli Carpenter, said the eggs were uncolored raw and cooked while the bread baked and she always ate the eggs.

So I really don't know what to tell you about the eggs. I guess the question is "To Eat or Not to Eat (the eggs)."

After searching the Internet cooking sites and the many of my cookbooks I finally found the recipe which I have tweaked. This sweet bread is not as airy as the Portuguese sweet bread, but quite tasty.

There was a comment in one of the cookbooks that said; "Nobody ever eats the eggs, but store the bread in the refrigerator just in case."

Easter Sweet Bread

8 tablespoons (1 stick) unsalted butter

1 teaspoons vanilla

½ cup milk

1 tablespoon grated orange or lemon zest

1 envelope (2 ½ teaspoons) dry active yeast

About 5 cups all-purpose flour

½ cup warm water(100° to 110° F)

1 teaspoon salt

3 large eggs, at room temperature

6 eggs, colored for Easter

½ cup sugar

1 egg yolk, beaten with 1 tablespoon water

Multicolored round candy sprinkles

Heat butter with the milk in a small saucepan just until the butter melts. Let cool. Sprinkle the yeast over the warm water. Let stand until the yeast is creamy, about 5 minutes. Stir until dissolved.

In a large mixer bowl, beat the 3 eggs until foamy. Beat in the sugar until blended. Add the butter mixture, yeast, vanilla, and orange or lemon zest. Add about 4 ½ cups of the flour and the salt, mixing until a soft dough forms. Gradually add just enough of the remaining flour to make a smooth, slightly sticky dough.

Turn the dough out onto a lightly floured surface and knead it for a minute or so, until it is very smooth. Shape dough into a ball. Butter a large bowl and place the dough in it. Cover with plastic wrap and let rise in a warm place until double in size, for about 1 ½ hours.

Butter two large baking sheets. Punch down the dough and cut into 4 pieces. Roll out one piece between your hands into a rope about 22 inches long. Repeat with another piece of dough. Lay the ropes side by side and loosely braid them together.

Lift the braid onto one of the baking sheets and bring the ends together to form a ring. Pinch the ends to seal. Place 3 of the whole eggs at intervals around the wreath, tucking them in between the ropes of the dough. Repeat with the remaining dough and eggs. Cover with plastic wrap and let rise into double in size, about 45 minutes.
Preheat oven to 350° Brush the dough with egg yolk mixture. Scatter the candy sprinkles on top. Bake for about 30 minutes, or until golden brown, reversing the position of the pan halfway through the baking time. Transfer the bread to racks to cool completely. Cut into slices to serve. *Makes 2 round loaves*

April 2010

I have been cooking and baking for most of my life, learning from my grandmother and mother at an early age. I remember my grandmother would give me some of the dough to roll out. I was so proud that I was helping her, when in reality she was keeping me quiet and out of her hair while she made the homemade (never store brought) macaroni for the family. During the first seven years of my life, we lived on the first floor, with my grandparents, great grandmother, aunts, uncles and cousins living on the other two floors of a house in Providence. Many of my other relatives lived within walking distance and our house was the center of all the family functions. I was always with my grandparents and I learned so many things from them. It is really amazing that although they spoke Italian, for the most part, and I spoke English, that I was able to absorb so much knowledge.

Terésa, Mom, Tanya and AnneMarie

My values of family, friends, hospitality, generosity and a love for good food are a direct result of growing up in that wonderful extended family. I learned to make the homemade macaroni, the soups, both the everyday meals and the special occasion meals, but I never learned to make homemade bread. Back in those days (just that phrase makes me feel so old!), we had fresh baked, still warm from the oven, bread delivered right to our door. So I never watched my grandmother or mother making bread. I have to admit that I have always been just a little intimidated by thoughts of making bread.

Well, on one of our many excursions to community events, I was introduced to a bread recipe that looked good and tasted delicious. This event happened to be at the Greene Public Library, where Sal is on the Board of Directors, and, lo and behold, the baker was none other but the librarian, Gail Mitchell-Slezak. Gail was nice enough to share her recipe with me. I was thrilled to learn that this recipe was for an almost no-knead bread. I decided to make the bread for a dinner party that I was having for some friends. I did of course change the recipe just a little bit.

Almost No-Knead Olive Bread

3 cups unbleached bread flour, plus additional for dusting the work surface
¼ teaspoon instant yeast
1 ½ teaspoons table salt
¾ cup plus 2 tablespoons water at room temperature
¼ cup plus 2 tablespoons of beer
1 tablespoon white vinegar
1 tablespoon fresh minced rosemary leaves
2 cups grated Parmesan cheese
1 cup of a variety of sliced green and black olives, rinsed
1 tablespoon muffuletta, drained (olive salad mix)

Whisk flour, yeast, Parmesan cheese, rosemary, and salt in large bowl. Add water, beer, and vinegar, olives and muffuletta. Using rubber spatula, fold mixture, scraping up dry flour from the bottom of bowl until shaggy ball forms. Cover bowl with plastic wrap and let sit at room temperature for 8 to 18 hours.

Lay one 12 by 18 inch sheet of parchment paper inside a 10" skillet and spray with nonstick cooking spray. Transfer dough to a lightly floured work surface and knead 10 to 15 times. Shape dough into a ball by pulling edges into middle. Transfer dough seam-side down, to parchment lined skillet and spray surface of dough with cooking spray.

Cover loosely with plastic wrap and let rise at room temperature until dough has doubled in size and does not readily spring back when poked with finger, about 2 hours. About 30 minutes before baking, adjust oven rack to lowest position, place 6 to 8 quart heavy-bottomed Dutch oven (with lid) on the rack and heat oven to 500.° Lightly flour top of dough and using sharp knife, make one 6 inch long, ½ inch deep slit along top of dough.

Carefully remove pot from oven and remove lid. Pick up dough by lifting parchment paper overhang and lower into pot. Let any excess parchment paper hang over pot edge. Cover pot and place in oven. Reduce oven temperature to 425° and bake for 30 minutes.
Remove lid and continue to bake 20 to 30 minutes longer until loaf is deep brown and an instant read thermometer inserted into the center registers 210°. Carefully remove bread from pot, transfer to wire rack and cool to room temperature, about 2 hours.

May 2010

These past few months have been very strange weather-wise, between the cold, snow, record setting rains, and the very few really beautiful days interspersed between the dreary ones. I, for one, am glad that spring has finally sprung and the flowers are blooming once more. I have to say that winter really got to me this year and I needed a break. I was craving some sunshine so I convinced Sal at the last minute to drive down to Florida to visit some friends, hoping to get in some sunshine and warmth in early March.

Who knew that this was the coldest, rainiest, watery winter that Florida has seen in forever? It was strange to drive through Virginia and the Carolinas and see snow! It was still a wonderful vacation, even if the weather didn't cooperate for us, because we got to visit with good friends. It's funny that even on vacation, I somehow end up cooking.

Many years ago, during our first visit to Florida, my friend, Gerry Tucker, introduced me to veal osso buco. It just so happens to be one of his favorite meals. He mentioned that he can no longer find it on the menu in the restaurants in Florida. I had just had a dinner party and had served osso buco (page 87) prior to leaving for vacation.

Here in Rhode Island, I can call Dave's or any other meat market and order veal shanks without a problem and at a reasonable price. In Central Florida, we had to call around to many markets and finally Anne and I drove 45 minutes to Orlando to Whole Foods to buy the veal and at triple the amount I pay here in good old Rhode Island. Veal osso buco is best served with risotto, another of Gerry's favorites. I had never made risotto before, thinking it was too difficult to make.

Well Anne and I searched the internet for risotto recipes. However, all the recipes that we looked at either had too many ingredients or not enough. So I looked for the technique to make the dish, checked out the ingredients in Anne's kitchen, and set out to make Gerry's favorite meal.

I ended up making risotto twice during our vacation, once for Gerry and Anne and then for our other friends, David and Doreen. It really isn't hard to make it just takes time to do it right. Here is the basic recipe that I culled from all the other recipes we looked at on the Internet.

The key to making Risotto is using the correct rice; you must use either carnaroli or arborio, which is an Italian long-grain variety. You can add other ingredients, like peas, or mushrooms or any other ingredients that suits your fancy. The following makes six servings.

Risotto

4 or 5 cups of chicken broth (either homemade or low sodium)
3 tablespoons butter
¾ cup chopped onions, or a combination of shallots and onion
1 ½ cups Arborio or Carnaroli rice
½ cup dry white wine, lukewarm
½ cups freshly grated Parmesan cheese
Pepper to taste

In a medium saucepan, bring the broth to a simmer and keep hot over low heat. In a large, heavy saucepan, melt the butter; add the onions and shallots and sauté until tender. Do not brown the onions.

Add the rice, stir to coat the rice with the butter and cook for a few minutes stirring the rice to prevent burning. Add the wine and simmer until it has almost evaporated. Add about a ½ cup of the simmering broth and stir until almost completely absorbed.

Continue cooking the rice, adding the broth at about ½ cup at a time. Allow each addition to absorb before adding more broth.

Remember to stir constantly until rice is tender, but still al dente (firm to the bite) and mixture is creamy. This process takes about 20 to 30 minutes.

Remove from the heat and add the Parmesan cheese and pepper, and other additional ingredients of your choice. Transfer the risotto to a serving bowl, top with a tablespoon of butter and serve immediately.

Add your own twist...

June 2010

Have you ever noticed that winter just seems so long and that spring takes forever to make its appearance? Then all of a sudden, spring is here, gone, and summer is just around the corner! It's already June, did we really have spring? Did I somehow miss it? I suddenly realized that I have to get busy because the Scituate Rotary Club's second annual wine & beer tasting event is scheduled for the 12th of this month!

So I and the committee have been busy, creating flyers, working with Alpine Wine & Spirits, who are providing the wines and beers, asking our wonderful merchants in town for items for the silent auction and ,of course, selling tickets.

The event is being held at the Edgewood Manor, a beautifully restored Greek Revival Mansion on Norwood Avenue in the Edgewood section of Cranston. If you ever want to get away, but not go too far, and stay in a beautiful bed & breakfast this is the place to go. In fact, come to the event and you can have the opportunity to bid on a one night stay in a magnificent room and have a wonderful breakfast, plus you get to try wines and beers from around the world.

In addition, to all the work that goes into planning this event, the final stages are deciding what food we will be serving our guests. Tina Vangel, Marie Carpenter and I are preparing the food for the evening and being Italian women we tend to go just a little overboard, so the hot and cold hors d'oeuvres will not be the typical fare.

So I thought I would share one of the recipes that I will be making that night, stuffed mushrooms. I like to use Portobello mushrooms as they are firmer, hold their shape and have a richer flavor. For an event like the wine tasting, I will look for mushrooms that are bite sized, for a dinner party; I will use a larger mushroom. The other thing about mushrooms is that you can stuff them with just anything, from crabmeat, sausage, cheese to a bread stuffing. This is my basic recipe for my stuffed mushrooms.

Micheline's Stuffed Mushrooms

Mushrooms
Bread crumbs
Chopped parsley (2 tablespoons if fresh or 1 ½ teaspoons if dry)
Minced garlic (about 2 cloves)
Grated Romano and/or Parmesan cheese
Chopped black olives
Finely sliced sun-dried tomatoes
Black pepper to taste

Preheat oven to 400° Wipe the mushrooms with a damp cloth, remove the stems and set aside. Spray a cookie sheet with olive oil Pam®; arrange the mushroom caps, cavity side up.

Finely chop the stems of the mushrooms and put in a medium sized bowl. Add your breadcrumbs, cheese, olives, and sundried tomatoes, garlic and parsley. Stir the mixture to incorporate the ingredients, add a drizzle of virgin olive oil and a little wine (whatever is available). You want the mixture to be moist to just enough hold together, but not so wet that is fall out of the mushroom.

Use a scant teaspoon of the stuffing to fill the cavity. Spray the mushrooms with a light coating of Pam® olive oil and bake until the mushrooms are still firm to touch, but not stiff.

Depending on the size of the mushrooms, the cooking time varies. I also did not list the amount of the ingredients because it depends on how many mushrooms you are making and the size of the mushrooms.

Once you have the mushrooms chopped, you should be able to judge how much breadcrumbs to add. (Just remember that you should taste the other ingredients, not the breadcrumbs.)

July 2010

In June, the Scituate Rotary Club held its second annual Wine & Beer Tasting and as one of the co-chairs, I was responsible for getting items for the silent auction. So a couple of weeks before the event I went into the village of North Scituate to some of my favorite stores to ask for donations.

My first stop: Cute as a Button. This is by far my most favorite store. Barbara has the greatest little things to fill creative baskets that can be tailored made to suit the occasion. Every present that I have bought there has been a hit.

On the day of the event, I was frantically trying to put the auction items together, make them attractive to the eye and appealing enough to elicit bids, when I suddenly remembered that I had yet to put together the Italian food basket. I tried to put all of these items in this basket, I really did try, but there was no way that I was going to make it work and look attractive.

Well, I just drove down to see Barbara, and I really didn't have to beg. She saved me by making two beautiful baskets, as well as donating a basket herself. I was saddened to learn that she is leaving our quaint village, but she's not going far, just down route 6 into Johnston. Please check out her store you will be surprised by what you will find.

Then it was into Bittersweet & Ivy, where I brought the cutest little ducks to add to my collection of cute stuff. Ede donated a beautiful painted plaque, with a candle and sign, to which I added a bottle of wine from Alpine Wine & Spirits and presto a great auction item. Again another great place to shop; I always find something that I cannot live without.

Next, I checked out one of the newest stores in the village called "Just Myrna." There I met the most delightful woman, who creates beautiful works of art with flowers. Myrna has a variety of different things in this cute building including organic lotions and soaps. She recently moved back to Scituate from Florida, so stop in and say hello, introduce yourself and welcome her back to little old Rhode Island. Check out her store, you will not be disappointed. Myrna also donated a gift bag of goodies.

Christine Hall from Charming Treasures donated a wine diffuser, coupled with another bottle of wine it became another great auction item. (See what you missed by not coming to the Rotary wine & beer tasting, not to mention the food.) Enchanted Yesterdays donated a tart warmer and a painted sign; I could wander in that store for hours looking at all the old and new items in all the nooks and crannies.

Further down the road, I wandered into Enza's Hair Studio & Day Spa. What a beautiful place. You just know by the décor that you are there to be pampered. I know that I am going to treat myself to some of the services, maybe for my birthday next month. Enza donated a gift certificate, so that lucky winner is in for a treat.

There was a beautiful painted mailbox, donated by Susan Sprague, Vangel's Jewelers donated a bracelet and pen & pencil set, the Corner Bistro a gift certificate, Angelic Image Designs (if you like my hair, see Maria) gifts certificates, just to name a few of the wonderful donations. Everywhere I went in Scituate, even with the tough economic times, the shopkeepers gave to the Rotary. I realized that if we do not support our local stores, they will disappear, and we will lose a vital part of what makes Scituate a great place to live. I, for one, would rather shop in these wonderful little places then at the malls, where everything is the same.

Anyway on to the recipe of the month, I made my Italian tuna, which we served in mini phyllo cups at the wine tasting. I may have mentioned before that I do not do mayonnaise at all, so my tuna salad is made with olive oil and balsamic vinegar and other things that you don't usually find in tuna salad. Ingredient amounts are to taste and adjusted to how many are being served.

Micheline's Italian Tuna Salad

A can of solid white tuna, drained, and flaked with a fork. Add to the tuna, chopped black & green olives, red onion, capers, chopped celery, and chopped yellow and red peppers. For a little heat, I add chopped pepperoncini peppers. To that I add a mixture of fresh spinach, mixed spring greens, and arugula, which I have chopped into small pieces.

Mix the ingredients together to distribute with the tuna, season with pepper and garlic to taste. Then I either add a reduced balsamic vinegar (I cook it down with a little sugar until it thickens) and extra virgin olive oil or I make the good seasons® Italian salad mix, using extra virgin olive oil and vinegar (it really doesn't make a difference what kind you use) which I put into the blender until it thickens. Add enough to keep the tuna together, but not too much that it is soggy.

Besides serving on a crusty roll as a sandwich, or filling a mini cup, I have also hollowed out a baguette and stuffed it with tuna, then you slice the bread and it makes a great appetizer.

My tuna can change with the ingredients that I have on hand at the time. Try it! I think that you will like it.

August 2010

August is here already, and summer is coming to an end. It's been a busy few months and I am enjoying the last of the warm weather.

Remember when you were a kid, you knew once August was here, soon after it was back to school. I miss those carefree days. I always spent most of the summer months at my grandparents summer home in Bristol, until the mid-sixties, when they sold the house and moved to Governor Francis Farms in Warwick.

Some of my best summer memories are from the Bristol days. On weekends, the whole family would congregate at my grandparents' house. It wouldn't just be all of the aunts, uncles and cousins; there would be the great aunts and uncles, and the second and third cousins too. It was like a family reunion most weekends.

We would dig clams and pick mussels and periwinkles off the rocks. Uncle Pete would always bring crabs. There would be homemade bread, pizza, macaroni, and my grandfather's wine. Grandpa would plant a huge garden, so we would have fresh vegetables.

I always felt special, because I, along with a few cousins would stay with them during the week too. I am going to share a bean salad recipe that is a nice summer side dish.

August 1952 -.My sister, AnneMarie Grossi, my grandma, Michelina Iantosco Bevelaqua, my Great-Aunt Fanny, and me at the beach in Bristol.

Bean Salad

1 can black beans
1 can black eyed peas
1 can shoe peg corn
1 can chick peas
1 small red onion, chopped
1 cup olive oil
1 cup sugar
1 cup apple cidar vinegar or white balsamic vinegar
1 tablespoon fresh chopped parsley
1 teaspoon fresh chopped thyme

Rinse beans and corn well. Mix corn, beans, and onions together; set aside.

In a saucepan, mix the olive oil, sugar, and vinegar and cook over low heat until sugar is dissolved. Pour over bean mixture and let sit overnight. Strain the mixture and toss with fresh herbs and pepper just before serving. Serve with tortilla chips or as a side dish.

August 1952 -.My sister, AnneMarie Grossi, my grandma, Michelina Iantosco Bevelaqua,
and me at the beach in Bristol.

September 2010

From the very beginning of my life with Sal, he has always had antique cars. In the 60's and 70's, it really wasn't all that unusual to drive around in old cars, because you could buy an everyday car for under a hundred dollars.

When I was in college, I bought a late model 50's Rambler for $50 bucks to get me back and forth to RIJC or "Reject" as it was known. The ignition was broken and battery terminals were corroded, so between having to hot wire the ignition and cleaning the battery terminals just to get it started, I can say without a doubt that the Rambler didn't qualify as an antique car. It was more of a junk car! Sal, on the other hand, drove a 1947 Packard Clipper.

Sal likes to collect and drive old cars, and during the years we have been together, there have been a few unique models in our driveway. It seems like yesterday when I had no idea that Packard, Hudson, Studebaker, Kaiser and Cord are cars, let alone know how to identify them. You may have seen us tooling around the town in our 1941 Cadillac 60 Special, with the wood trim.

Anyway, along with the car hobby there are car clubs to match the type of car you own. So being the kind of people who have nothing to do, we joined the Yankee Wood Chapter of the National Woodie Club, a club for people with wood bodied cars or an appreciation for the "Woodie". The YWC is more of a social club with a wonderful group of people, who enjoy each other's company and have fun driving our cars.

We have made so many friends and I owe it all to Vickie DeLuca, who was so persistent in including us in club activities. Thank You, Vickie. The last week in June, Sal and I hosted a mini tour for our club. We had billed it as a "Tour to Nowhere". At some point in the planning stage it became a "Tour to Somewhere". The rendezvous point was the State Police Headquarters, and lining up were Annette & Brian with the 1949 Packard Station Sedan, Nat & Cathy in their 1973 Corvette, David & Judy in a 2009 Shelby, Al & Nancy looking good in the 1953 Buick Wagon, and Arlene & Albert (minus their 1967 Chevelle, (which, the day before, decided it needed a new starter, that's what happens to those old cars) riding with us in our 41 Cadillac.

Our first stop was at Glocester Greens and Goats to visit with Carolyn and Ray. While Ray checked out the cars, we checked out the goats and gardens. We saw the most adorable baby goats, Carolyn gave us the opportunity to bottle feed them after which they followed us all around the yard. Arlene, a real city girl, wanted to take a baby goat home with her. Carolyn treated us with samples of her wonderful goat cheese and we tasted her garden of unusual greens. Do you know there are plants that taste just like root beer?

After a last minute quick good-bye to the baby goats (and Carolyn and Ray, too) we traveled on to Woodstock, CT to tour a historic mansion. Roseland Cottage, Bowen House is an 1846 Gothic Revival style house. The complex includes an ice house, aviary, carriage barn with private bowling alley (which is reported to be the oldest in the country), and Victorian parterre garden. Since the Bowen family lived in the house until donating the property to the Historical Society, it still has all of the original furnishings.

We then toured the back country roads in Connecticut returning to our house for a lunch. I had ice cold lemonade, Italian potato salad, green bean salad, marinated grilled chicken, and a new recipe for grilled pork. It was a hit, so I thought I would share it with you. This recipe serves 4.

Grilled Pork Tenderloin with Rosemary Mustard Rub

4 stems of fresh rosemary
3 cloves garlic, peeled
4 tablespoons of extra virgin olive oil
2 teaspoons cracked black pepper
1 teaspoon coarse sea salt
3 tablespoons of a stone ground mustard
1 lb. of pork tenderloin

Remove rosemary leaves from stems and place in a small food processor with garlic, oil, salt, pepper and mustard. Pulse until the mixture resembles a paste. Smooth over pork, place on a baking sheet, cover, and refrigerate for at least 30 minutes.

Preheat grill to high, brush the grate with oil. Sear pork on each side for about 3 minutes. Reduce heat to medium low, close the cove of the grill and cook pork for about 8 to 10 minutes or until the internal temperature registers 145°

Jack & Vickie DeLuca's Grandson - Future Chef of the DeLuca Family - Photo from Glen Photo.

Transfer pork to platter, let rest for about 5 minutes, slice and serve. I have also roasted this pork in 325° oven instead of on the grill and it comes out just as tasty, but with a different texture.

October 2010

Have you ever noticed that as you get older your perspective on life changes? I remember growing up and hating the idea of going to wakes. I thought it was so barbaric, this practice of seeing someone lying in a coffin. Of course, it made no different what I thought, my parents expected me to go with them to pay my respects and you did as you were told. As I grew older, I realized that wakes were a time to see family and friends and share memories.

When my father died, I really appreciated that my friends, co-workers, and acquaintances came by to express their sympathy. It touched me that they cared. In August, death came three fold to my family; a cousin-in-law one week and the following weekend, my aunt and first cousin. August, like October, has become a bittersweet month with both wonderful and heart-rending memories.

I have to share my Aunt Lou with you. Lucrezia Bevilacqua was one of those rare individuals, who opened her heart and home to whomever came to her door. She never judged, or uttered an unkind word. Her family came first, and most importantly she loved unconditionally. I have many aunts, with my mother being one of eight and my father being one of nine children and I love them all. However, my Aunt Lou held a very special place in my heart. Aunt Lou was married to my mother's brother, Joe, but she was more like a sister than a sister-in-law to my mother.

No matter what time of day or night, you happened to find yourself at her door, she would put on the coffee, set the table and take out the food. No one ever left Aunt Lou's home hungry! She treated everyone like family, whether it was the first time she met you or the fiftieth time.

I remember going to her house one day when she and a neighbor were making meatballs (in large quantities) for a church supper. She was baking the meatballs on a cookie sheet instead of frying them and I thought, "What a great idea." I quickly learned to oven fry my meatballs, chicken cutlets, and eggplant, it's less work and healthier.

At the wake, my cousins and I shared stories about Uncle Joe and Aunt Lou, we checked out who had more gray hair (those of us who have gone au natural), caught up on what we have been doing, and shared pictures of children and grandchildren. We laughed and cried and talked about having a family reunion. It just doesn't seem right that the only time we see each other is at wakes.

I, apparently, have been designated by my cousins to take the lead on planning such an event. This will be a major undertaking as the Bevilacqua and Iantosco families number close to 300.

When we were younger, every year we had a family reunion and my Aunt Lou would always make her brownies. She always used boxed brownie mix and frosted them. When my cousin Michele asked me why they were so good, I told her it was because Aunt Lou made them with love. She will be missed, but never forgotten.

So in honor of my Aunt Lou, I would like to share my brownie recipes. The first is my mother's blond brownie and the next is my brownie recipe with chocolate frosting.

Blonde Brownies

1 can sweetened condensed milk
½ cup chopped walnuts
1 10 oz. package chocolate bits
24 graham crackers, crumbled
1 tablespoon melted shortening

Mix ingredients together and pour into a greased 11"x7" pan, bake in 350° oven for about 20 minutes. Cut into squares while warm.

Left: October 1947 - Uncle Joe and Aunt Lou on their wedding day in Providence. **Right:** Aunt Lou in her kitchen in Warwick.

Add your own twist...

Chocolate Brownies

1 cup oil
⅔ cups cocoa
2 cups sugar
½ teaspoon baking powder
2 teaspoons vanilla
½ teaspoon salt
4 eggs
1 cup flour

Blend oil, sugar and vanilla in a bowl. Add eggs, one at a time, beating well with a spoon. Combine flour, cocoa, baking powder and salt. Gradually add dry ingredients to the mixture.

Spread in greased 15 x 10-inch pan. (For thicker brownies, bake in a 13x9 inch pan.)

Bake at 350° oven for 15-20 minutes or until brownie pulls away from the pan. Cool and then frost.

Chocolate Frosting

2 tablespoons milk
1 cup sifted confectioners' sugar
½ teaspoon vanilla
3 tablespoons unsweetened cocoa

Stir the sugar and cocoa gradually into the milk, add the vanilla and stir until mixed. You may have to add more sugar is the frosting is not thick enough.

November 2010

Is it just me, or does it seem that the older we get, the faster time seems to go? I can't believe that 2010 is almost over, it's already November (really, it's the middle of October as I write this column), I just finished decorating the house for the Fall Season and before you know it, Fall decorations will need to be switched to the Christmas décor. It must have been the unseasonably warm weather, but I really had a difficult time switching gears to get ready for autumn. I must admit that I had to buy this wonderful witch's hat to provide the motivation to drag up the container of witches, scarecrows, pumpkins and black cats. I have a confession. There are times that I invite guests or plan a party just to provide the motivation to change my seasonal décor. Actually, now that I think about it, I probably saved money just buying the witch's hat.

In addition to my lack of seasonal motivation, I apparently have a case of writer's block and for the past two weeks (Carol, I do try to get the column written before the deadline, really I do!) I have been thinking of what recipe to share and story to tell. Maybe it's a golden moment or a power outage that is causing my brain to freeze. Since I have just rationalized buying yet another decoration and along the lines of economizing, this year I plan to make some homemade treats to give as gifts.

I always make cookies, lots and lots of cookies, and give trays as gifts. Since making cookies (lots of cookies) for the holidays can cause my brain to freeze, I play Christmas music to get in the mood.

I make cookies for the beginning of December for our party; then I start over again just before Christmas for the other festivities. Several years ago, I decided not to make quite so many cookies and gave presents instead of the cookie trays. I have to tell you that idea went over like a lead balloon; everyone was looking for the cookies. Like my grandmother and my mother, I am destined to make cookies until I'm in my nineties.

Anyway, with the economy still in the pits, I decided to be a little old fashioned and make something else in addition to the cookies to give to family and friends. This first recipe is for sweetened condensed milk, which is used in cookies and fudge recipes. It's not something to give away, but it's simple to make, costs pennies, and makes enough for three cups. The other recipes are for mixed nuts. I plan to pack them in festive containers; add some candy bark (page 72) and maybe a bottle of homemade liquor (Bailey's®, Kahlua®, or limoncello) and presto! Nice gifts, made with love, and economical too.

Sweetened Condensed Milk

½ cup butter-flavored shortening
2 cups granulated sugar

2 cups powdered milk
1 cup boiling water

Place ingredients in a blender and process until smooth. Refrigerate in a covered container. Mixture will thicken as it stands. One cup plus 2 tablespoons, equals the 15 oz. can that most recipes require. This recipe makes 3 cups.

Sweet & Crunchy Nuts

¾ cup pecan halves
¾ cup walnut halves
½ cup whole blanched almonds
1 egg white, lightly beaten

⅓ cup SPLENDA® no calorie sweetener, granular
2 teaspoons ground cinnamon

Preheat oven to 300° Spray a 15- x 10- x 1-inch pan with cooking spray. Combine pecans, walnuts, and almonds in a mixing bowl; add egg white, tossing to coat. Combine SPLENDA® granular and cinnamon; sprinkle over nuts, tossing to coat. Spread mixture evenly in prepared pan. Bake 30 minutes or until nuts are toasted, stirring every 10 minutes. Cool on waxed paper. Store in an airtight tin.

Toasted Rosemary Pecans

4 cups pecan halves (1 lb.)
4 tablespoons unsalted butter, melted
1 ½ teaspoons salt

1 teaspoon dried rosemary, lightly crushed
½ teaspoon sugar

Preheat the oven to 250° Spread the pecan halves on a large rimmed baking sheet. Bake them for 15 minutes, shifting the baking sheet halfway through for even coloring, or until they are lightly toasted. Drizzle the melted butter over the pecans, then sprinkle with the salt, rosemary and sugar and toss to coat. Bake the pecans for 15 minutes longer, shifting the pan halfway through, or until browned and crisp. Transfer to paper towels and let cool.

December 2010

In my family, Christmas Eve was the special night for the family to gather for Feast of the Seven Fishes, although we never called it by that name. Thinking back, I'm not sure that we prepared seven fish dishes. We always had little necks on the half-shell, snail salad, a kind of fish stew made with stuffed squid, mussels, little necks, and fish, in a spicy tomato sauce.

Of course, there were fried smelts followed by shrimp and spaghetti. Dessert consisted of the many varieties of cookies. After dinner we would open some presents and the kids would be sent to bed to await the arrival of Santa Claus.

On Christmas Day, we would visit the relatives not present on Christmas Eve. We would return home to have dinner that would consist of antipasti, chicken escarole ('Shcarole) soup and lasagna. Now I have to tell you, we have never called this soup Italian Wedding Soup, although it was often served at weddings. My mother would make this soup every Monday night minus the meatballs (that was only for special occasions). Monday night my Aunt Lottie and Uncle John came over for soup and to play cards. I always make my own broth, cooking the chicken, with garlic, celery, onions, lemon peel, and cinnamon stick.

December 1983 - My brother-in-law, Frank Lombardi on Christmas Eve in Woonsocket.

Chicken Escarole Soup with Little Meatballs

1 large head of escarole
6 quarts of homemade chicken broth
4 carrots, shredded
3 hard-boiled eggs, mashed

For the mini meatballs:
½ lb. ground veal
2 eggs
½ cup unflavored breadcrumbs
3 tablespoons, chopped parsley
¾ cup grated Parmigiano or Romano cheese
red pepper flakes to taste

Mix all the ingredients for the meatballs together, make into dime size balls. I pan fry them in olive oil as I like them firm; however you can also cook them in the soup.

Trim the escarole, and discard any bruised leaves. Cut off stem ends, separate leaves and wash well. Cut the leaves into bite size pieces. Put the escarole, carrots, and broth in a large pot and cook until escarole is tender.

Stir in the meatballs and small macaroni like acini di pepe and boiled eggs and simmer about 20 minutes. Serve with grated Parmigiano or Romano cheese.

My Aunt Lottie Grossi Riccitelli And Uncle John Riccitelli

January 2011

Throughout the years I have belonged to many organizations, some are still near and dear to my heart, some I look back and say "what was I thinking?" some I just aged out of and moved on to bigger and better things (or more mature groups). My experience being a member of the YWCA of Greater Rhode Island changed the course of my life. My membership in the Yankee Wood Antique Car Club expanded the group of people that I have the privilege to call friend. Membership in the Scituate Rotary Club brought me fun, fellowship, and service above self as well as more friends.

Through the Rotary Club, I had the honor of knowing Norman Smith. Norm, a retired history professor from RIC, was the president of the Scituate Rotary Club during my second year as a Rotarian. He had the most delightful sense of humor and with his wry wit he would poke fun at some of what I call the "Grand Pooh Bah" that often comes with large organizations. I thoroughly enjoyed talking with him as he had a wealth of knowledge as well as a thirst to learn more. Since this past year he was in failing health, he was accompanied by his personal chauffeur, his wife, Lola. I always call Lola 'the lovely Lola,' as she is just a very special woman.

It was a sad day when I heard that Norman had passed away. The memorial service was held at the Mathewson Street Methodist Church in Providence on a Sunday afternoon and the Rotary provided the food for the collation. Tina Vangel and I (along with our husbands, Tina's mother and my sister) were to get to the church early to set up, while other members of our club would be bringing more food and refreshments.

Now you would think that driving into downtown Providence on a Sunday afternoon would be a "piece of cake," but not that afternoon! The streets of Providence were blocked off for a road race, with the church right smack in the middle of the road closures. We were told in no uncertain terms that the road was closed and would not reopen until 12:30 pm, which was just the time that the service was to begin.

Panic was setting in; there was no way we could walk several blocks with all the stuff we had to bring with us. Then I had a brainstorm, since I am the supervisor of probation at the Providence District Court and I work closely with the Providence Police, I just so happened to have a Detective Lieutenant's cell number in my phone.

As luck, or perhaps divine intervention, would have it, Bob was working the traffic detail at police headquarters that day. I explained the problem and he, in turn, contacted the officer controlling that street, and suddenly the barriers came down for us to enter and I became the hero of the day. I know what you're thinking, what does this story have to do with food? Well besides setting up, I made pizza and, since I always make pizza for our Christmas Party, I thought I would give you the recipe.

Just so you know, I do not make the usual tomato and cheese pizza, I am very creative with my toppings. I have included the recipe to make the dough, but you can cheat (I often do) and buy the dough. Make sure that it is Italian bread dough; I go to the bakery for mine. If the dough is cold let it warm up to room temperature, as it is easier to work.

Basic Pizza Dough

Ingredients:
2 ½ tablespoons fresh cake yeast or 1 package dry yeast
1 cup lukewarm water
Pinch of sugar
1 teaspoon salt
3-3 ½ cups unbleached white flour

Warm a medium mixing bowl by swirling some hot water in it and drain. Place yeast in the bowl, pour on the warm water. Stir in the sugar, mix with a fork and allow to stand until yeast has dissolved and starts to form, about 5 - 10 minutes.

Use a wooden spoon to mix in the salt and about one third of the flour. Mix in another third of the flour, stirring with the spoon until it forms a mass and begins to pull away from the sides of the bowl.

Sprinkle some of the remaining flour onto a smooth work surface. Remove the dough from the bowl and begin to knead it, working in the remaining flour a little at a time. Knead for 8-10 minutes. By the end, the dough should be elastic and smooth. Form into a ball.

Lightly oil a mixing bowl. Place the dough in the bowl. Stretch a moistened, wrung out dish towel across the bowl and leave it to stand in a warm place until double in volume; about 40-50 minutes.

To test whether the dough has risen enough, poke two fingers into the dough. If the indentations remain, the dough is ready.

Punch the dough down with your fist to release the air. Knead for 1-2 minutes.

If you want to make two pizzas, divide the dough into two balls. Pat the ball of dough out into a flat circle on a lightly floured surface. With a rolling pin, roll it out to a thickness of about ¼ inch.

If using a pizza stone, roll out the dough on corn meal so that you can slide the dough onto the stone with a pizza peal. If using a cookie sheet, roll out the dough on a lightly oiled pan.

Preheat oven to 475° for at least 20 minutes before baking. If using a pizza stone preheat the stone in oven. I like using my pizza stone best, but for large gatherings, I use cookie sheets as it is easier to cut the pizza into uniform pieces.

Bake the pizza about 15-20 minutes or until the crust is golden brown.

I always add the mozzarella (or a combination of Italian shredded cheeses) about 5 minutes before the pizza is done. I season the toppings with pepper (red or black), basil, fresh or powdered garlic and oregano. Pizza can be a great starter to any party, with any choice of toppings.

Me and my great-great-niece Iszabella in the kitchen.

As to the toppings, a basic cheese and tomato or pizza alla Margherita use either fresh or canned tomatoes, crushed, grated Parmesan cheese, fresh basil leaves (torn into pieces), olive oil and pepper to taste.

I often use pesto as a base, with sliced fresh tomatoes, black olives, mushrooms, parmesan and mozzarella cheese. I will also use an olive tapenade, roasted red pepper & cheese spread, artichoke spread or brushetta spread as a base.

Add grilled vegetables, sliced pepperoni, sliced artichokes, sliced zucchini, cooked sausage (sliced or crumbled) or whatever you would like to top the pizza.

Add your own twist...

February 2011

On January 15th my mother, Mary Bevelaqua Grossi, turned 97 years young and my brother, sister and I decided that it warranted a celebration. Since we knew that she would not agree, we decided not to tell her. What can I say? We can be just a little sneaky when we need to plan a surprise!

It wasn't a big party, we couldn't invite the whole family and host of friends since then we would need a very large hall (just immediate family with all the cousins and their families numbers in the hundreds). My brother, Joe, invited her to spend the weekend and when she noticed that my sister-in-law, Barrie, was making a few appetizers she became a little suspicious.

When Sal and I arrived with more food, she started to ask questions, but I assured her that it was no big thing; just a few people were coming over.

I knew the gig was up when her cousins Etta and Joanie (whom she had not seen in a while) walked into the house and she was just so surprised. Right behind them was her sister, Due, who rarely leaves her house. That's when my mother became overwhelmed with emotion.

My mother is the oldest of eight children, having three sisters and four brothers, my Aunts Helen, Due and Tessie and my Uncle Leo are still with us. Only my Aunt Helen was unable to be there to help her celebrate this momentous occasion.

It was wonderful that my niece, Lori, who lives in Utah, and has been visiting for the past two months helping my sister, AnneMarie, while she recuperates from a broken hip, was here for the celebration. Several of my cousins and most of my mother's great grandchildren were on hand for the party as were my childhood friend, Arlene, and her husband, Albert.

My Uncle Leo, who is deaf, (having lost his hearing during combat in the Korean War, (he was awarded the Bronze Star) kept trying to remember who these relatives were.

Cousin Joan Iantosco D'Ambrosia, Mom, Uncle Leo, Aunt Tessa, and cousin Etta Iantosco Braun

Arlene has been a friend since we were 11 years-old and has often attended our family reunions, and she looked familiar to Uncle Leo, but he had no clue as to who she was.

Having a conversation with Uncle Leo is a challenge as you really have to yell. At one point, he remarked to me that he didn't realize that my husband was so big (Sal is 6 feet tall). I told him that Sal wasn't really that big; it was just that we are all short.

It was a fairly small party, with about 40 people in attendance, and we had decided to have appetizers and a variety of sandwiches. My niece, Lori, (her birth made me an aunt at the age of nine) decided that I should make my new recipe for an appetizer meatball and since I have had several requests for that same recipe, I have decided to share it this month.

I have a couple of friends who have Celiac disease, which is an allergy to gluten, and I decided to experiment with making a meatball without bread. The results turned out to be a success. So here is my recipe for my veal, sausage and gorgonzola meatballs.

Veal Gorgonzola Meatballs

1 lb. ground veal
1 lb. of Graziano's hot sausage (or any other extra lean good Italian sausage)
8 oz. of gorgonzola cheese, crumbled
1 cup cooked rice (either white or brown)
Eggs or egg beaters
Fresh parsley, minced garlic, pepper to taste
Balsamic fig glaze

Remove the sausage from the casing and mix with the ground veal. Add the gorgonzola cheese and the rice and mix well. Add enough eggs or egg beaters to make a soft meatball.

It should just hold together and be really moist. Add the parsley, garlic and pepper and mix well. Make the meatballs the size of a small walnut and drop on a cookie sheet sprayed with cooking oil.

Bake at 425° for about 5 minutes and then turn them around and bake for another five minutes or until brown. Drizzle with the glaze, or serve the glaze on the side. These meatballs might also be good with a gorgonzola cream sauce.

(Note you can buy Graziano's sausage at Dave's Market)

March 2011

I was looking out my window at the snow and listening to the icicles falling from the roof and I had a flash-back. I felt like I was in the back seat of the family car and asking my parents that age-old annoying question: "Are we there yet?" Except, I was thinking is it Spring yet?

Valentine's Day has just passed and the temperature outside today reached the low 50's, but I don't know when the last of the snow is going to disappear. The weatherman (or weatherwoman) said colder temperatures and another snowstorm is on its way. At this rate, the kids from "no-school Foster-Glocester" will be going to class in August.

Tonight I attended the Scituate Preservation Society lecture on the history of dairy farming in Rhode Island. It was interesting to learn that, at one time, Scituate was one of the largest farming areas in the state. Did you know that during the days before refrigeration and modern transportation that Rhode Island exported butter and cheese?

The things you learn in the country! I have always associated dairy farms with milk as the main product, but without refrigeration and a fast means to bring milk to market, the milk would spoil, so instead these ingenious farmers made cheese and butter to sell. Salt was used as a preservative. Rhode Island butter and cheese was sold as far away as the Caribbean Islands and was a valuable commodity.

March 2015 - Passing on traditions with my niece, Tanya, my great niece Jade and my great great niece Iszabella.

It was an interesting lecture which provided insight into what life was like before all of our modern conveniences. Anyway, once again the Scituate Rotary teamed up with the preservation society and provided a pot luck dinner before the lecture. It's one of the perks, when the president of the society is married to a member of the Rotary. I decided to make a baked macaroni dish for the pot luck.

Baked Macaroni with Artichokes and Olives

This recipe is very versatile since you can change the type of macaroni, the vegetables, the meat and the sauce.

1 lb. of Rigatoni- cooked very al dente- under cooked by a couple of minutes.

To make the sauce, heat 2 to 3 tablespoons of olive oil over medium heat. Add a small diced onion, a shallot cut into thin slices; and one diced red pepper, and red pepper flakes and cook until the onions and shallot are softened. At this point add about four cloves of garlic, and cook until garlic is golden in color.

Once the vegetables are cooked add a 28 oz. can of crushed tomatoes (I always puree the crushed tomatoes in the blender with fresh parsley and basil) and 1 can of plum tomatoes, pureed. Simmer until the tomatoes darken in color and the sauce has thickened, which takes about 20 to 30 minutes. Season the sauce with fresh chopped basil, parsley and more red pepper flakes if you want it spicy.

Those of you who know me realize that I have given you a recipe for a red sauce and not gravy. In my family our gravy is seasoned with meat drippings and thickened with tomato paste and slow-cooked for hours. (Which answers the question : "Is it sauce or is it gravy?")

I add two cans of quartered artichokes and 8 oz. of sliced black olives. You can use about 3 cups of any cooked vegetables, like zucchini, eggplant, escarole, or cooked meatballs or crumbled cooked sausage.

Add 1 cup of fresh ricotta to your sauce, mix the macaroni and vegetables, and add 3 cups shredded provolone, mozzarella, asiago or fontina cheese and 1 cup of grated Parmesan or Romano cheese.

Toss the macaroni and vegetables with the sauce and half of each of the cheese. Spread in an oiled 3-4 quart baking dish. Sprinkle the remaining cheese over the mixture and bake uncovered in a 350° oven for about 30 minutes until heated through and browned on the top.

April 2011

Finally, winter is behind us and spring is right around the corner. Although, as I look out my window, I can still see snow. Since it is Lent, Sal and I just had dinner at the North Scituate Fire Station; it's their annual fish and chips every Friday in Lent fundraiser. So how did the practice of eating fish on Fridays start?

I remember growing up Roman Catholic and we always had to have fish on Friday or it was a sin. During Lent, we had to eat fish or rather not eat meat on Wednesdays and Fridays. At some point, the rule was changed and it was just during Lent that it became fish on Fridays.

I decided to Google the question and found some interesting comments. They ranged from the ridiculous to something that sounded like it made sense. The comment that made the most sense to me is as follows:

"In the first century, Jews fasted on Mondays and Thursdays. The original Christians were all Jewish and were used to the fasting as a spiritual discipline. They moved the fast days to Wednesdays and Fridays, because Judas engineered Jesus' arrest on a Wednesday and Jesus was crucified on a Friday.

Most often that fast took the form of avoiding meat in the diet. In those days, meat was a luxury food. You either had to buy it in a market or you had to own enough land to keep cattle. On the other hand, anyone could grow vegetables or forage for them, and anyone could catch a fish in a lake or a stream. You could buy better fish and vegetables, but the point is that you could eat without money if you were poor. So meat was rich people's food and fish was poor people's food. That is why the most common form of fasting was to omit meat and eat fish." --This is from Karl Loren Happiness' website.

I don't know who he is, but I thought what he had to say fit what I remember and seems to be historically feasible. Anyway, back to eating fish or rather not eating meat during Lent. My mother would always make dishes like pasta e fagiole, shrimp and spaghetti or spaghetti aioli. I would like to share a recipe that I adapted from *The Italian American Cookbook*. This recipe serves four and has sweet and sour flavors. It works well with any firm flesh fish.

Swordfish Agrodolce

¼ cup pignoli (pine nuts)
Salt, preferably sea salt
¼ cup extra virgin olive oil
Fresh ground pepper
2 med. yellow onions, thinly sliced
3 tablespoons chopped Italian parsley
¼ cup dry white wine
(4) 6 oz. swordfish steaks
¼ cup red wine vinegar
Flour for dredging
½ cup balsamic vinegar
3 tablespoons olive oil

Heat a small skillet over medium heat. Add pignoli and cook, shaking the skillet often, until the nuts are toasted. This takes about 5 minutes. Remove from heat and set aside.

Heat a medium saucepan over medium heat and ¼ cup olive oil. Add onions and cook, stirring until onions are golden brown, about 10 minutes.

Add the wine, and both vinegars, and salt and pepper to taste. Bring to a boil, then reduce heat and simmer until the sauce is reduced by half. Add parsley and the toasted pignoli, stir and remove from the heat. Season the swordfish with salt and pepper.

Dredge the fish in the flour, shaking off the excess. In a large sauté` pan, heat 3 tablespoons of olive oil over medium -high heat, add fish and sauté for about 2 minutes on each side. Do not overcook.

Quickly reheat the sauce and serve it with the swordfish. The swordfish should not be too thick for this recipe or you will need to cook it longer.

May 2011

April was a period of introspection for me; it was a time to explore the direction my life was going during its next phase. It was the month I made some life changing decisions. After much thought and consideration, I decided after 29 years to retire from state service. I had come to the crossroads of my professional career in corrections and wanted to make a change. It is a bittersweet decision, as I enjoy the challenges of mentoring staff and supervising offenders (I have always liked working with criminals).

In recent years I am privileged to be in a leadership role in the changing direction of probation and parole. I will miss that challenge. I will miss being on the cutting edge of the prisoner re-entry. I will miss working with the Providence Police Special Victims Unit and the community agencies that service the offender population. I will miss working with these dedicated detectives, professionals and probation and parole officers, who every day make a difference in the lives of victims and the offenders. I will miss the problem solving with the court personnel, police, prosecutors, attorneys, and last, but certainly not least, the judges. That is to say, I will miss the hustle and bustle that is The Providence District Court.

So although I am retiring, I know that I need to find something else to do with my time. If I win the Powerball, I will travel to Italy and Europe, but since the odds are somewhat astronomical, I don't really foresee world travel in the near future. So short of winning the lottery or having a long lost fabulously wealthy relative leaving me their fortune, I will need to find another career to stimulate my mind and keep me in pocket change.

I have another month or so to explore career possibilities that I can use my passion for writing, cooking and mentoring. Since both Sal and I are retiring, I will now have time to make nice leisurely breakfasts. Here is a recipe for baked peach French Toast which is just that kind of breakfast. I decided to check the internet to find out if French toast was really French. Here is what I found: French Toast is called "pain perdu" in French. Perdu means lost, because the bread used was mainly stale bread. Another source said no, it was invented in Belgium and there were dishes similar to it in ancient times.

Baked Peach French Toast

Six 1-inch thick slices whole-grain bread
8 oz. cream cheese
6 sliced medium fresh peaches
½ cup chopped pecans
½ cup whole milk
½ cup buttermilk
⅓ cup maple syrup
3 large eggs
2 tablespoons unsalted butter, melted
1 tablespoon sugar
1 teaspoon cinnamon
1 teaspoon vanilla extract
1 tablespoon Kahlua® coffee liqueur (optional)

Pre-heat the oven to 400° Lay bread slices in a casserole dish or other baking dish. Prick bread 3 to 4 times each with a paring knife and spread a layer of cream cheese on top of each slice of bread. Arrange peach slices on top of bread slices to cover bread. Sprinkle nuts over peaches.

Combine remaining ingredients well. Pour over bread, trying not to dislodge nuts too much from top of peaches. Bake 20 to 30 minutes, or until bread is no longer "soggy" and just begins to brown on the edges.

You can assemble the French toast and let it sit in liquid for several hours or overnight in the refrigerator before baking. Cored and peeled apple slices may also be substituted for the peach slices.

June 2011

Well it's now official; as of July 1ˢᵗ I will be a retired person! I have been spending the last few weeks, attempting to clean out my office of the various items one accumulates over 29 years. I found myself wondering why I saved half the things that I discovered in my desk and file cabinets. I have distributed my many colored paperclips, push pins and magnets to my wonderful and supportive clerical staff, without which I could not do my job so well. Meagan, who is the princess of pink; Laurie, who loves the color purple; Stephanie, the dark and beautiful blues; Jessica, the powdered blue items and to Ali, the reds and orange to match her hair. They must think me completely nuts, have too much time on my hands or really appreciate that I separated all the clips and push pins by color for them.

Since I knew that this was my last administrative assistant day, I tried to pick out just the perfect (color coordinated, of course) gifts for them. Naturally I found just the perfect items for my gift bags in the Scituate village shops. Each member of my staff has received a memento from me that, I hope, will elicit fond memories of their supervisor. I wondered if their next supervisor will make them a frittata, Irish bread, carrot cake, or homemade candy for the staff meetings.

Although I know that I will not miss the stress of the courthouse, lack of staff to supervise the many offenders in Providence, the vacant caseloads or the politics of dealing with administration, I will miss the people and the challenges of the job.

It is now the time to come up with new challenges (without the criminal element that has been present for the last 29 years) as I move on to the next stage of my life. Before my final departure from Providence District Court probation, I will have a farewell staff meeting and make them a blueberry sour cream coffee cake. Perhaps, you can make it for your office.

Blueberry-Sour Cream Coffee Cake

2 cups all-purpose flour
1 tablespoon baking powder
½ teaspoon salt
2 sticks (½ lb.) unsalted butter, softened
1 ½ cups granulated sugar
2 large eggs, at room temperature, lightly beaten
1 cup sour cream
1 tablespoon pure vanilla extract
¾ cup blueberry preserves, plus 1 tablespoon melted preserves
Confectioners' sugar, for dusting

Preheat the oven to 350°. Butter and flour a 10-inch Bundt pan. In a medium bowl, whisk together the flour, baking powder and salt. In a large bowl, beat the butter until creamy. Add the granulated sugar and beat until fluffy. Beat in the eggs, sour cream and vanilla. Beat in the dry ingredients just until incorporated.

Spread all but ½ cup of the batter into the prepared pan. Using the back of a spoon, make a trough in the batter, all the way around the pan. Mix the ¾ cup of blueberry preserves with the reserved batter and spoon it into the trough.

Bake the cake for about 1 hour, or until it begins to pull away from the pan and a skewer inserted in the center comes out clean. Let the cake cool in the pan for 15 minutes.

Invert the cake onto a wire rack, remove the pan and let cool completely. Sift the confectioners' sugar over the cake, drizzle with the melted blueberry preserves and serve.

July 2011

It's July and the first month in 29 years (actually more like 45 years if you count the time I started working at sixteen) that I do not have to get up and go to work. It is definitely going to be a big change. I am looking forward to the adjustment of my lifestyle. June was a very busy month starting with the end of a wonderful 50's cruise where we partied with our friends, "Reminisce," from Boston to Bermuda and back again. The last time, Sal and I were on a cruise was 32 years ago for our honeymoon, also to Bermuda.

Anyway, we got back on the first Friday and immediately I started to put the finishing touches of the program for Bill Vangel's Installation as the District Governor of Rotary District 7950 and the next President of the Scituate Rotary Club, Jeremie McLaughlin, which was on the second Friday. After that I started working on the Rotary's Wine Tasting and Beer Sampling that was held at the end of the month. In between, I cleaned out my office, said my goodbyes to my staff and court personnel, and attended my retirement party.

That was June! Now it's July and I don't seem to be slowing down a bit! On July 4th the Rotary will host their Pancake Breakfast at the Community House during "Old Home Days". Thank you, God! I do not have to cook for that event; I manage the dining room and help with the prep work instead.

July 1970's - My mom, Mary Grossi, and my Uncle Mike Bevelaqua at his birthday party in Warwick.

Then, a few weeks of rest and I'm back cooking for the 19th annual Greene Public Library Chicken BBQ on July 24th and then there is the Lombardi Family Reunion the last week in July. I thought retirement was supposed to give you more time. When do I get to rest?

Anyway, I decided to make "Caponata ai Capperi" or Caponata with Capers, which is like an eggplant relish that can be used as an antipasto, to use on bruschetta, or a side dish. Here is the recipe for your enjoyment.

Caponata ai Capperi "Eggplant Relish"

Ingredients:
4 tablespoons extra-virgin olive oil
1 ¼ lbs. eggplant, diced into ½-inch cubes
1 ¼ lbs. red and yellow bell peppers, cut into ½ -inch pieces
2 garlic cloves, thinly sliced
½ cup tomato puree
¼ cup red wine vinegar
1 tablespoon sugar
3 tablespoons salt-packed capers, rinsed, soaked in cold water for 10 minutes, then rinsed again
1 teaspoon whole green peppercorns, optional
Freshly ground black pepper and Salt
Flat-leaf parsley sprigs for garnish

In a large heavy nonstick skillet, heat 2 tablespoons oil over medium-high heat until hot but not smoking. Add eggplant, in batches if necessary, and a pinch of salt; cook, stirring occasionally, until tender, 5 to 7 minutes. Transfer to a large bowl.

Add remaining 2 tablespoons oil and peppers to skillet. Cook, stirring occasionally, until peppers soften, about 10 minutes; add garlic and cook, stirring, 1 minute more. Stir in tomato puree, capers and peppercorns, if using. Reduce heat to medium, cover and cook, stirring occasionally, until peppers are tender and flavors have blended, about 10 minutes.

Meanwhile, in a small saucepan, bring vinegar and sugar to a boil; cook until reduced by half, about 5 minutes. Remove from heat.

Transfer pepper mixture to bowl with eggplant, stir in reduced vinegar, and season to taste with salt and pepper. Serve warm or at room temperature, garnished with parsley.

August 2011

The other day my sister, AnneMarie Grossi, and I were reminiscing about growing up in Providence in our extended family household. Our home was a triple-decker right near Rhode Island Hospital on Borden Street. We lived on the first floor, our grandparents, great grandmother and unmarried aunts and uncles lived on the second floor, and the third floor was occupied by our Aunt Angie, Uncle Peter and their family.

There was a grapevine covering most of the backyard and a small garden at the rear. I was lucky to have had my grandparents in my life, to be able to learn from them about our culture, our food, and our heritage. I was 13, when my great grandmother, Antonetta Iantosco (we called her Mamadona) ,died at the age of 87, and 15, when my grandfather, Michele Bevelaqua, died at the age of 75. Fortunately, my grandmother, Michelina Bevelaqua, was in my life for 35 years. She was 91 when she passed away.

I was exposed to the old world traditions, and learned to cook the old fashioned way… we never opened a can of beans, we soaked the dry beans and cooked them. Use a cake mix? That was unheard of! We made our cakes and cookies from scratch. Back then, my grandmother baked her own bread and made our macaroni (not pasta). Now that I am retired, I am going to be making breads more often; that is, once the weather turns cooler.

AnneMarie and I are animal lovers; we always had dogs and a parakeet while growing up. If my sister could rescue all the hurt animals in the world, she would. One day, my grandfather found a pigeon with a broken wing and took it home. AnneMarie decided to nurse it back to health. She bound up the wing, fed it every day and put it in a box on the third floor fire escape. Soon it was fat and healthy, but not quite ready to fly. Every day she would come home from school and check on her patient. Then one day, the patient had disappeared! AnneMarie ran downstairs and asked Mamadona where her pigeon was, and she replied that it had flown away (flown the coop!)

Well, AnneMarie just didn't believe it, so she opened up the refrigerator and saw this tiny plucked bird. She looked at Mamadona and said, "what this?: Mamadona replied "it's a little chicken."

You see, in the old country, squab (i.e.pigeon) is a delicacy. I have found many recipes for squab in my Italian cookbooks, but somehow I could never bring myself to try making any of the dishes.

Sal has raised Fantail and Jacobean pigeons, so it would be like eating a pet, ugh! So instead, here is a recipe for another "little chicken," Cornish Hens. You can find

Cornish Hens right in your neighborhood supermarket. The recipe is Cornish Hens alla Diavolo. The term fra diavolo means "brother devil" and it is a fiery, spicy, pepper dish; alla diavolo means "devil's style." The recipe serves two to four and can also be grilled.

Left: *My sister, AnneMarie Grossi, at the age of 10.* **Below:** *My uncles, Mike and Pete Bevelaqua, with my great grandmother, Mamadona Antonetta Iantosco in the early 1960's.*

Clockwise -Top Left: *August 1951 - My first birthday at our home on Borden St. with my sister Anne-Marie, brother Joe, Aunt Tessi, Grandma, Great Grandma and assorted cousins* **Top Right:** *1982 - My dad, Joe Grossi, was never without his hook. Kids would point and call out, "Captain Hook!".* Center *Right: Iszabella in her red jacket playing in the snow.* **Lower Right:** *1942 - Joe Grossi, my dad, honeymooning in New York City.* **Lower Left:** *Christmas 1980 Woonsocket - My mom, Mary Bevelaqua Grossi and my nephew, Frank Lombardi.* **Center Left:** *1940's - My stylish aunt and uncle, Mike and Helen Bevelaqua.* **Center:** *September 1958 - Miki Lombardi posing for my first communion on Beaufort Street.*

Cornish Hens alla Diavolo

2 Rock Cornish hens, rinsed and patted dry
2 tablespoons Italian parsley
2 tablespoons extra-virgin olive oil
Juice of one lemon, and one lemon, quartered
2 teaspoons of sea salt or kosher salt
1 tablespoon coarsely ground black pepper

Cut each Cornish hen in half from neck to tail and remove the backbone. Press down on the halves to flatten them. Place them in a shallow bowl, and toss them with olive oil. Season them with the salt, pepper, parsley and lemon juice. Cover with plastic wrap and refrigerate from 4 to 6 hours.

Preheat the broiler. Remove the Cornish hen halves from the marinade (reserve marinade) and place them, skin side up, in large roasting pan. Broil 6 inches from the heat for about 10 minutes, brushing occasionally with the marinade during the first 5 minutes. Turn the hens over, brush once with the marinade, and broil another 5 minutes. Turn off broiler and set oven for 425°

Turn the hens skin side up and roast for another 8 to 10 minutes until done. Arrange the hens on a platter and drizzle with olive oil.

September 2011

This summer reminded me of the summers of long ago; that time when school was out and you were too young to have a job. It reminded me of my carefree youth and summers spent with my grandparents. During the early 1950's, my maternal grandparents owned a summer home in Bristol, Rhode Island, not too far from the RI Veteran's Home and within a short distance from the ocean.

The house was small, just three bedrooms, one bath, kitchen and living room, but it had a wonderful screened in porch that went three quarters off the way around. It was also built without a cellar, which didn't sit well with my grandfather. So he decided to dig the cellar out from underneath the house. It was great; it was all dirt, with a low ceiling and just perfect for wine making and keeping the barrels of wine at the perfect temperature. There is nothing better than homemade wine directly from the barrel!

I pretty much spent the entire summer with my grandparents, with various cousins visiting all the time. Every weekend we would all go to Bristol, aunts, uncles, great aunts and great uncles, first, second and third cousins, as well as friends to visit with my great grandmother and grandparents. Since the porch went around the house, cots were set up to sleep, with a sheet dividing the boys from the girls.

If it was a weekend overflowing with family, some of the youngest were delegated to the attic, which was not as much fun since it tended to be hot and could only be reached by pulling down the stairs. I was lucky as I was able to stay there most of the summer with my cousins, Mary Ann and Michele. Mary Ann was lucky, as her maternal grandparents lived up the street from us and she got to stay with her mother's side of the family as well.

Bristol was where my grandfather, Michele Bevelaqua, taught me about the ocean. He would talk about his home in Provincia di Foggia, Italy, which is on the Adriatic Sea. He would point out the various creatures of the ocean. On the weekends, we would go down to the water and pick periwinkles (we called them penny winkles) and mussels off the rocks, and dig for clams and quahogs.

There were times when there were close to a hundred people there on Sundays and most weekends there was an average of 50 relatives and assorted friends. So, we needed to go the ocean to supplement feeding the family.

I remember being in Bristol, walking with my grandfather on the beach right before the 1954 hurricane. It was so quiet; the sea was still and there were no seagulls flying around. It was just eerie. He told me it was because a storm was coming and we needed to return to Providence. It was during Hurricane Carol that my sister taught me how to tie my own shoelaces; I had just turned four years old. Summers in Bristol were the best times of my life.

I was privileged to spend quality time with my grandfather, who gave me a love of the sea and a taste for wine, and with my grandmother and great grandmother who taught me about food and the importance of family, and knowing so many of my assorted relatives.

So today I'm going to give you a recipe from the sea; Zuppa di Cozze which translated means Mussel Soup. It is really mussels in a spicy sauce. This recipe serves four, but can easily be adjusted to serve many more or you could use little necks or a combination of both.

August 1939 - Grandpa Michele Bevelaqua coming up from the cellar in Providence with a jug of his homemade wine.

2013 - *My mom, Mary Grossi, my sister, AnneMarie Grossi, me, my niece, Tanya Bledsoe, great-niece Jade Capobianco and Isza-bella Baily, my great - great - niece at our family reunion at Goddard Park.*

Zuppa di Cozze "Mussels"

4 lbs. mussels
4 garlic cloves, finely chopped
2 tablespoons chopped fresh parsley
1 small onion, chopped
⅓ cup olive oil
1 cup wine, red or wine
2 large cans of Italian tomatoes, drained and chopped
Crushed red pepper to taste

Place the mussels in cold water to cover for about 30 minutes, drain and scrub them with a stiff brush. Scrape off any seaweed or barnacles, discard ones with cracked shells or any that do not shut tightly when tapped. Remove the beards by pulling them toward the narrow end of the shells.

In a large saucepan, cook the garlic, onion, parsley and crushed red pepper in olive oil until the garlic is golden. Stir in the wine and bring to a simmer, then add tomatoes and cook over medium heat, stirring occasionally until the sauce is slightly thickened, about 20 minutes.

Gently stir in the mussels. Cover the pot, Cook until the mussels open, about 5 to 10 minutes. Discard any shells that refuse to open. Serve with garlic bread.

October 2011

Last month there was a notice in the Providence Journal noting that on September 6, 1901, President William McKinley was shot during the Pan-American Exposition in Buffalo, New York. My cousin, Netta Iantosco DiSanto called my mother and jogged her memory that their Grandfather, Giuseppe Iantosco, was there when the President was shot.

When my mother told me about the incident, I was curious enough to research the assassination and discovered that it was after McKinley's death that Congress passed legislation charging the Secret Service with protecting future Presidents' lives. It was an interesting piece of personal history to learn that my Great Grandfather was present at this history making occasion. It prompted me to ask my mother questions about him since he died a long time before I was born. I learned that he traveled throughout America, visited Yellowstone National Park, worked fabricating steel and owned a variety store in Providence. He also wanted to move the family from Providence to Cranston near Roger William Park, but Mamadona didn't want to "move way out to the country."

I also have been going through some old photographs in anticipation of using some in my next project, publishing a *Mangia with Micheline Cookbook*, and came across one of my grandfather. It was taken at one of our family reunions, which were held every year until the late 1960's. All the female cousins would meet every month during the year and plan the summer outing. I'm not really sure why the reunions stopped, but I know several of my cousins keep looking to me to start them up again. I've been known to plan a few parties in my time.

October 1961 - The children and spouses of my grandparents.

Since a reunion for my family would mean a gathering of around 250 people, I suggested that it is more than a one person venture. I keep waiting for some of the younger cousins to step up to the plate and offer to help. Maybe next year will be the year for the Iantosco-Bevelaqua Reunion. So, since I am being sentimental, I thought I would share a favorite cookie recipe with you. My mother would often make molasses sugar cookies for the family.

Molasses Sugar Cookies

¾ cup shortening
2 cups flour
1 cup sugar
½ teaspoon ground cloves
¼ cup molasses
½ teaspoon ginger
1 egg
1 teaspoon cinnamon
½ teaspoon salt
2 teaspoon baking soda

October 1961 - My grandparents, Michele and Michelina Bevelaqua at Stella D'Italia Restaurant in North Providence celebrate their 50th anniversary.

Melt shortening in a small pan over low heat, remove from heat and let cool. Once the shortening is cool add the sugar, molasses, and egg and beat well.

Sift together the flour, baking soda, cloves, ginger, cinnamon, and salt. Add the dry ingredients to the first mixture and beat until all the ingredients are mixed together.

Chill for at least one hour. Form the mixture into 1 inch balls and roll in granulated sugar. Place on greased cookie sheets about 2" apart. Bake in a 375° oven for 8 to 10 minutes.

..

November 2011

My husband has a sign on the wall of our rumpus room that reads: "Every October, Hershey; the rest of the year is just waiting." And so it is that every October we start on our pilgrimage to the largest antique car event in the world.

This year we took a side journey to visit Bill and Paulette Mack, who have relocated up near Erie Pennsylvania, before going on to Hershey. Bill made a wonderful white Pasta e Fagiole (I'm going to have to hit Bill up for his recipe) and I made the discovery that I like white cannellini beans as long as they are al dente. So thank you Bill! That discovery has opened a whole new variety of recipes to share in the future.

Anyway, October is the month of pumpkins, scarecrows, and things that go bump in the night. Right next door to Hershey Park is Hummelstown, a charming place, whose main street reminds me of Scituate Village. During the whole month of

October, the street is lined with scarecrows, designed by the locals businesses and organizations. People vote for their favorite scarecrow, and the styles ranged from a family of skeletons named The Bone Family sponsored by the chiropractor, a scarecrow made up of paint cans from whom else but a painter, and one stuffed with play money from the bank. It is one of my favorite stops during our annual trek to the land of chocolate and car parts.

October is a beautiful month, with its trees painted with color and doorsteps decorated with pumpkins and mums. So what do you do with all those left over pumpkins? Let's face it how many pumpkin pies can you bake or eat! I have this great recipe for Pumpkin Cake, which my niece, Terésa, gave me many years ago. She hand wrote the recipe and drew a picture of a cake on a stand. You know that's a recipe that I will keep forever! Here is the recipe complete with the cute drawing.

Sal performing Monster Mash at Foster Old Home Days

Pumpkin Cake

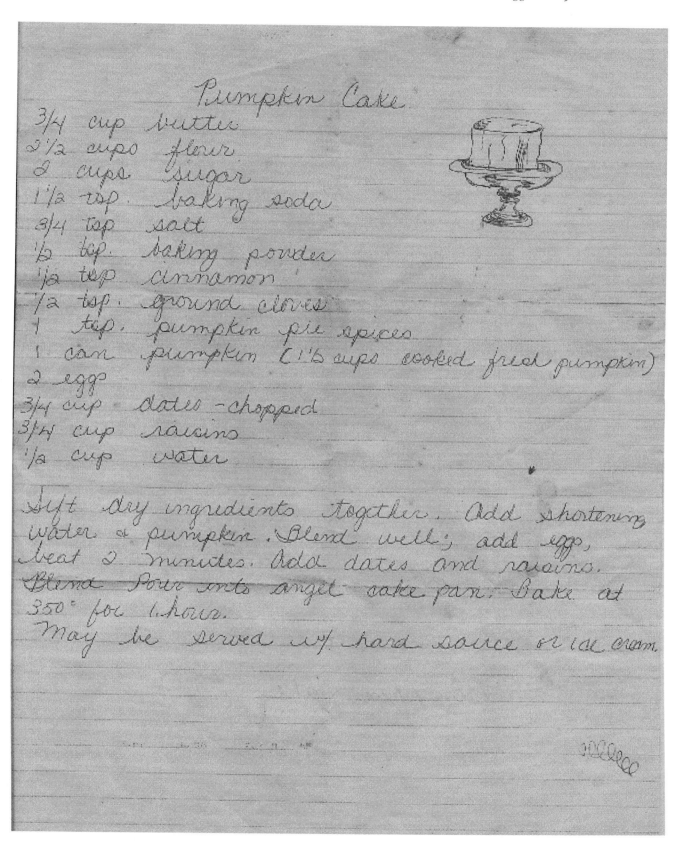

3/4 cup butter
2 1/2 cups flour
2 cups sugar
1 1/2 tsp. baking soda
3/4 tsp salt
1/2 tsp. baking powder
1/2 tsp. cinnamon
1/2 tsp. ground cloves
1 tsp. pumpkin pie spices
1 can pumpkin (1 1/2 cups cooked fresh pumpkin)
2 eggs
3/4 cup dates - chopped
3/4 cup raisins
1/2 cup water

Sift dry ingredients together. Add shortening water & pumpkin. Blend well; add eggs, beat 2 minutes. Add dates and raisins. Blend Pour into angel cake pan. Bake at 350° for 1 hour.

May be served w/ hard sauce or ice cream.

December 2011

It is December already! My favorite holiday is just around the corner. It is Christmastime and I get to deck the halls, bake mountains of cookies, wrap pretty presents and cook for hordes of people. What could be better than that?

Every year I try to decorate the house just a little different. I guess it would help, if I took pictures of the rooms, so I could remember how they looked in the past but, lo and behold, that would be just too easy. My problem is that I have too much 'stuff' that I have collected or have been given throughout the years and not enough rooms for all the decorations.

This year I decided to go for a completely different look and instead of a large real tree, I have several smaller trees in a few rooms. It's funny, but growing up, the Christmas tree was the main focus with just a few other decorations around the house. I suppose it had to do with the fact that our parents were products of the Great Depression and life was less complex. The holidays were more about family, friends and great food than gifts or decorations.

We often gave homemade gifts of food or clothes. One year, when I was in high school, I decided to make my three nieces these cute red corduroy jumpers. I think my mother had me rip out the seams a hundred times before I managed to get it right. It also ruined me from ever making clothes again! I'd much rather make homemade treats any day.

Since I'm now retired and I am supposed to have more time to do things (I really haven't found that elusive time yet!), I have decided to make some liqueurs, candy and spiced nuts to give to my family and friends.

Here is my recipe for Kahlua®. There is still time to make some, find some pretty bottles and give a homemade treat!

"Kahlua®" Liqueur

4 cups boiling water
3 ¾ cups sugar
2 oz. instant coffee (measured in a measuring cup)
1 vanilla bean, split
1 quart of 100 proof vodka

Make simple syrup by boiling the water with the sugar for 5 minutes.

Remove from heat and add the instant coffee; bring back to boil and cook for 5 minutes.

Add vodka and split vanilla bean and pour into 1 gallon bottle; store in the dark for 2 weeks.

Add your own twist...

January 2012

I was really under the misconception that once I retired I would have so much time on my hands that this holiday season would be a snap. Now, I wonder how I managed to get anything accomplished while I was working.

Apparently, I do not know how to bake cookies during the daylight hours. I am still baking into the wee hours of the early morning. I guess, like my mother, I'm a night person. This month my mother is turning 98 years old and she can still be found baking cookies at midnight. It's just not Christmas unless she bakes cookies and gives away trays as gifts.

Anyway, now that the season is over, I am really going to buckle down and start on the next phase of my life. After consulting with Barbara Stetson, Scituate's cookbook connoisseur, I discovered that writing a cookbook will take a little more time and work than I anticipated. Winter will be a great time to stay at home and work on my *Mangia with Micheline* cookbook. Hopefully, I will be able to put it all together without driving myself crazy in the process.

My other plans for the future include cooking lessons and children's tea parties. Keep your eyes open as I will advertise in the *Foster Home Journal* (where else?). As for the recipe for this month, I thought I would give you something simple, but tasty since I imagine we are all tired after the Holidays.

This recipe is for crispy baked scallops. It serves four and takes under 30 minutes to prepare and cook.

Crispy Baked Scallops

Ingredients:

¾ cup Panko (Japanese bread crumbs)
2 tablespoons unsalted butter, melted
1 ½ teaspoons extra-virgin olive oil
¼ teaspoon dry mustard
½ teaspoon red pepper flakes
1 garlic clove, minced
1 tablespoon chopped flat-leaf parsley
1 tablespoon snipped chives
¾ teaspoon chopped thyme leaves
1 teaspoon chopped basil leaves
Salt and freshly ground black pepper, to taste
12 jumbo sea scallops (1 ½ lbs.)
Lemon wedges, for serving

Preheat the oven to 400° Lightly butter an 8-inch square baking dish.

In a small bowl, mix the Panko with the melted butter, olive oil, dry mustard, red pepper flakes, garlic, parsley, chives, basil and thyme. Pat the scallops dry and season with salt and pepper. Set them in the prepared baking dish and sprinkle the scallops evenly with the mixture.

Bake the scallops for about 10 minutes, or until barely cooked through. Turn the broiler on and broil the scallops 3 inches from the heat until the topping is crisp and golden brown, about 1 minute. Serve with lemon wedges.

February 2012

I discovered that the origins of Valentine's Day began around 269 A.D. in Rome. It is said that a Roman priest named Valentine died a martyr because he refused to renounce Christianity and he continued to unite lovers with holy vows of matrimony. His actions resulted in his imprisonment, where it is said he struck up a friendship with the daughter of his jailer. It was said that Valentine corresponded with couples he married as well as with the jailer's daughter. Of course this occurred in the days before instant messaging and texting.

Legend has it, that on the day of his execution, February 14th, 269 A.D., he left a final letter for his love and signed it "From your Valentine." The legend grew in Italy and in Europe and in 496 A.D. Valentine was honored with sainthood. His day of martyrdom became the day to celebrate love and lovers. In Italy, with its romantic and religious roots, St. Valentine's Day became the traditional day to be engaged.

Another interesting fact that I discovered in my computer search is why red roses are a symbol of Valentine's Day. It is said that red roses represent the intensity and passion for that special someone that you love and the heart represents love in purest form.

In addition, if you rearrange the letters in the word rose, you get Eros, who is the God of Love, better known as Cupid. Boy, the things you learn on the Internet!

My father, Joseph Grossi, used to give my mother, Mary Bevelaqua, beautiful Valentine cards and heart shaped boxes of chocolates. I never really thought of my father as a romantic figure as they were not the kind of a couple to be always kissing and hugging, but looking at the wonderful cards and the beautiful hearts, I realize that his was a romantic soul. I have two of the Valentine boxes that he gave her during the 1940's and I display them during February.

Now, I am very much my father's daughter as I love chocolate and it was always a mystery to me why Dad would buy chocolates for my mother, when she does not share this passion. Sal, like my mother, is not overly fond of chocolate and often complains that restaurants only have chocolate desserts on the menu. So it is a challenge to come up with a non – chocolate dessert for our romantic dinner.

I have decided on a dessert from the Piedmont section of Italy, and it is said that this dessert was created in the golden environment of the Court of Savoy—Zabaglione, Italian custard. It is considered one of the most famous of all Italian puddings. It is usually served in glasses, either hot or cold, and eaten with a spoon. I plan on serving it with sliced strawberries. The basic recipe is for each egg yolk, you will need a tablespoon of sugar and 2 tablespoons of Marsala wine, you may also flavor the pudding with grated lemon or orange rind, vanilla, or a liqueur.

Zabaglione

4 egg yolks
4 tablespoons sugar
8 tablespoons Marsala wine

In the top container of a double boiler, put in the egg yolks, over simmering, not boiling, water, add sugar and beat until very pale and fluffy.

Add the Marsala a little at a time and keep beating with a whisk or blending speed of an electric beater until the mixture thickens to the consistency of a light batter. This should take about 10 minutes. Set the pan in a basin filled with cracked ice.

Beat zabaglione until thoroughly cold. Pour into stemmed glasses and refrigerate, add the sliced strawberries right before serving.

My grandparents,
Michele and Michelina Bevelaqua,
all dressed for a wedding!

Zabaglione can also be served warm immediately after thickening in the double boiler.

March 2012

Retirement is a very different state of mind then working for a living. When working, I would get up every morning, look in my closet to determine what to wear, coordinate my makeup and jewelry, fight the traffic into Providence, deal with staff, police, court issues and, of course, the offenders. Every day was a different challenge and it was both stressful and exhilarating at the same time. It's not as if I really miss the rat race of working, but I miss the thrill and the people.

While I have a new challenge of working on my cookbook, Sal found some other projects to keep him busy. He has been clearing the yard and working on his personal museum. When we moved to our home, there was a gardening shack in the back yard, which, for a number of years, held an assortment of junk. I suggested that we should clean it out and use it for storage for our gardening stuff.

Well, we did clean it out and then Sal decided to take it over and make it into an old fashion filling station and farm store. It has a Gulf Gas pump from the 30's, an air pump, a kerosene pump, wide white wall tires, a horse drawn plow and a variety of advertisement signs adorn the outside of the building. Inside there is an old fashion pay phone, an old cash register, a variety of farm equipment, old Gulf maps, an old railroad desk, oil cans and God only knows what else he has on the shelves.

Sal will go into his filling station, which I affectingly call his man cave, fire up the kerosene stove to read the newspaper and listen to talk radio. When friends stop over, they can play checkers just like in the old days. After spending the morning in the filling station, he comes into the house to a warm home cooked lunch. One of my favorite winter stews is veal and peas. This recipe will serve four.

di vitello e piselli "Veal and Peas"

4 tablespoons olive oil
1 lb. of veal, cubed
1 small onion, diced
flour seasoned with salt & pepper
2 cloves of garlic, crushed
½ cup white wine
Hot pepper flakes, to taste
14.5 oz. can diced tomatoes, pureed
1 tablespoon fresh parsley, finely chopped
1 cup of frozen baby peas

Dredge the veal in seasoned flour. Heat olive oil in a heavy casserole, sauté onions until translucent, add veal and cook until brown.

Add garlic, red pepper flakes, parsley and cook until garlic just starts to get golden. Add the white wine to deglaze the pan, cook until liquid is slightly reduced. Lower heat, add tomatoes and cook slowly until veal is tender, add peas and cook a few more minutes. Add more wine if more liquid is needed. Serve with Italian bread.

Sal converted our shed into a filling station/farm store.

April 2012

Did you ever wonder why so many Italian Americans are New York Yankee fans? It all has to do with how many Italians played for the Yankees during 1930s through the 1950's. Everyone knows about Joe DiMaggio "the Yankee Clipper," and Yogi Berra, but let's not forget Joe Di Gangi, Vic Roschi, Billy Martin and, of course, Phil Rizzuto, "the voice of the Yankees." Since the New York Yankees had so many Italians on their team, compared to the Red Sox, it became the team of choice. From the year 1920 through 2003, the Yankees won 26 World Series and 39 pennants. Well, I am a New York Yankee fan, as was my father before me; in fact the majority of my family are Yankee fans.

However, my Aunt Tessie, Theresa Bevelaqua Cotta, is and has always been a diehard Red Sox fan. Aunt Tessie is my mother's youngest sister, with 20 years between them. Being the youngest of eight and the only Red Sox fan, she was subjected to a lot of teasing.

During the 1949 season, the Red Sox found themselves up by one game, with two games left against the Yankees for the pennant race. The game was going to take place at Yankee Stadium. My father and mother, my Uncle Leo and Aunt Frances Iantosco, and my Uncle Armando and Aunt Due DeCesare went to New York for the weekend to see the game. My Aunt Tessie was just a teenager at the time and she was convinced that it was the year the Sox were going to beat the Yanks, as they only needed to win one game. Knowing my aunt, I'm sure she made her opinion known!

Well the Sox lost 5-3 on the last day of the season after losing 5-4 the previous day, resulting in the Yankees winning their 16th American League pennant and they then went on to defeat the Brooklyn Dodgers in the 1949 World Series for their 12th World Championship. The story goes that my Aunt Tessie had to hide when my parents returned from their trip to avoid all their teasing.

So what does this story have to do with food? I decided, in honor of the baseball season, I would share my recipe for meatballs, after all they are round.

Go Yanks!

Go Sox!

Micheline's Meatballs

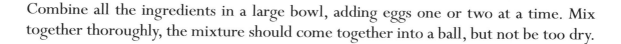

1 lb. of a mixture of ground beef, veal and pork
½ lb. of hot or sweet sausage, remove the meat from casing
¾ cup plain bread crumbs
4 to 6 eggs
2 to 3 cloves of garlic, minced
3 tablespoons finely chopped fresh flat-leaf parsley
¾ cups freshly grated Romano and/or Parmigiano cheese
Red pepper flakes to taste

Combine all the ingredients in a large bowl, adding eggs one or two at a time. Mix together thoroughly, the mixture should come together into a ball, but not be too dry.

Shape the mixture into 2-inch balls. Traditionally, we would fry the meatballs, browning them on all sides before adding them to the gravy, but I oven fry them. I spray a cookie sheet with cooking spray, place the meatballs on the sheet and bake them for about 10 minutes on each side in a 375° oven. It's faster and healthier.

Top: *Sal in a Yankees jersey at the PawSox.* ***Above:*** *My Aunt Theresa Bevelaqua Cotta, my Uncle Leo Bevelaqua and my mom, Mary Grossi.*

May 2012

I have been blessed to have many friends: friends from my earliest years in school, college friends, work colleagues, friends that I inherited from Sal, friends that share an interest in antique cars, in exotic poultry, antiques and doo wop music. It seems that our circle of friends continues to grow as we meet new people and enter into new ventures. I started to think about why some people that you meet become friends and some just remain acquaintances. I came to the conclusion that it has to do with shared values and cultural heritage.

Last month, Sal and I were visiting our friends, Pat and Barbara Bria. Now we met the Bria's through our friends, the DeLuca's, who are members of our car club. Vickie DeLuca grew up with Pat Bria, whom she calls Max, a childhood nickname. The first time I met Max and Barbara I was very confused because, Vickie kept calling him Max and his wife kept calling him Pat. [Sal and I decided he is more of a Max than a Pat] Max and Sal share a love for doo wop music and we have become great friends.

The DeLuca's and the Bria's grew up in Connecticut and our paths would never have crossed if not for antique cars and doo wop music. During our last visit, Barbara was telling me about her father, Joseph Nicastro, who was her family's historian. Like many Italians, he shared his stories and life lessons around the dinner table. His parents emigrated from Bari, Italy, which is in the Puglia region near the Adriatic Sea. Barbara shared the following story.

During the Great Depression, her dad received a call from his brother-in-law, Elmer Farrell. Now, Uncle Elmer was married to her father's sister, Lena. Her father was a stone mason by trade and he and his brother built the family home. During the Depression, they were young, strong and motivated and they held many jobs to help support the family and put food on the table.

Uncle Elmer had the only truck in the family, and he was called by a local store to deliver merchandise. Needless to say, her father and uncle set out to deliver for this store. That's how Joseph Nicastro and Elmer Farrell became the first delivery men for Sears and Roebuck in Norwalk, Connecticut.

I am going to share a recipe from the Puglia region of Italy in honor of Barbara's father. Puglia is especially known for macaroni called orecchiette. The name, orecchiette, means little ears because they resemble the human ear in shape. This recipe is for orecchiette and olives and serves 4.

Orecchiette and Olives

1 lb. orecchiette pasta
6 oz. pitted Kalamata, chopped
5 tablespoons virgin olive oil
2 clove garlic, crushed
3 tablespoons minced parsley
1 tablespoon tomato paste diluted in 2 tablespoons water, or 4 tablespoons tomato sauce

Heat pasta water, salt it and set the orecchiette to cooking. In the meantime, sauté the garlic in the olive oil, add the olives, and continue to simmer. When they have cooked somewhat, stir in the tomato and continue to simmer.

Drain the pasta, and add to the sauce. Stir the pasta until coated , if too dry add a little of the pasta water. Place in a bowl, dust it with the minced parsley, and serve.

December 2012 - Patrick Bria (Aka Max),
singing with Street Corner Serenade.

June 2012

My mother's youngest brother, Michael Bevelaqua, was movie-star handsome, with dark curly hair, big brown "bedroom" eyes and the best personality. One of my first and most vivid memories, when I was about 4 years-old, is seeing Uncle Mikey in his Navy uniform. He enlisted in the Navy during the Korean War and served on the USS Leyte, an aircraft carrier. In fact he was aboard the ship in October 1953, while it was in Boston Harbor undergoing conversion to an anti-submarine carrier, when an explosion claimed the lives of 37 sailors and injured another 28 men.

Every time I watch the 1949 musical "On the Town" staring Frank Sinatra and Gene Kelly, I think of Uncle Mike. Only he was better looking than Frank Sinatra and more dashing in his Navy whites. He gave me one of his sailor hats that I wore all the time when I was a kid. My uncle, unlike his many nieces and nephews, never went gray and we were always teasing him about using hair dye. I mean really-we were all in our 20's and 30's and had salt and pepper hair and his was still curly and dark.

Uncle Mike has always lived with my grandparents. During the first 7 years of my life he lived upstairs from me. After my grandparents sold the house in Providence, and moved to Bristol, they stayed year round at the summer home. Then in the early 60's, my grandparents sold the house in Bristol moved with Uncle Mike and his wife, Aunt Arline, to their new home in Governor Francis Farms in Warwick.

Uncle Mike shared the love of working in the yard with my grandfather, so the yard was a palette of beautiful flowers. Of course there was always a vegetable garden as well. His other love was playing golf, and he always had a foursome with his brothers, Pete, Joe, and Leo. Uncle Mike was a very special man, he loved his brothers and sisters and all his nieces and nephews, he took care of his parents and he was always there for his family.

We lost him in 1996 at the young age of 65, and I was privileged to give his eulogy. I remember looking out at the packed church and saying that although Mike Bevelaqua was not a wealthy man, he was very rich because he was so loved by his family and his many friends. I often think of him when I make a favorite recipe or watch golf on TV. Uncle Mikey taught me many things and one of the recipes that I learned from him I would like to share with you this month. I was about 10 years old, when he taught me how to make potatoes croquettes, using leftover mashed potatoes. Since I never have left over mashed potatoes, I have added some ingredients to make them company ready.

Patata Crocchetta "Potatoes Croquettes"

1 ¼ lbs. potatoes (I like Yukon Gold) peeled and cut into chunks
¼ cup combination of grated Pecorino and Parmigiano cheese
2 or 3 large eggs
1 tablespoon chopped fresh Italian parsley
¼ cup chopped ham (prosciutto, salami, prosciutto cotto, or cooked ham, any or a combination)
Pepper to taste
¼ teaspoon grated nutmeg
Flour
1 cup Panko or unseasoned Italian bread crumbs.
Olive oil for frying

Bring water to a boil and add potatoes and cook until easily pierced with a paring knife, about 15 minutes. Drain the potatoes, and while still hot either mash or put through a potato ricer.

While the potatoes are still warm, add the cheeses, 1 egg, parsley, ham, and spices. If the mixture is too dry add the other egg. Mix well. Flour your hands and take about ⅓ cup of the potato mixture and form into a small cylinder shape.

Roll into flour, dip in a beaten egg, and roll in the breadcrumbs. Set on a plate until all the potato mixture is used.

My Uncle Mikey, handsome in his Navy uniform while serving in the Korean War.

July 2012

My mother's only surviving brother; Leo Bevelaqua, will turn 84 this month. In honor of his birthday I would like to tell you a little about him. Uncle Leo is the prank-ster of the family.

For instance, when he was playing golf with his brothers, he would switch their good golf balls with ratty ones. Uncle Leo was always playing pranks on his siblings, like telling his sister Helen, that her fiancé, who served in the Navy during World War II, was on the phone for her. Of course, my Grandparents didn't have a phone, so Aunt Helen would run to her brother Pete's house several streets away only to find out that there was no call from Joe Badessa.

When I was a little girl, I spent a lot of time with Uncle Leo and his wife, Aunt Rita. They used to take me everywhere. Then in 1954, my cousin Michael Leo was born, followed by Paul, and finally Michele, and then Peter; so I was no longer Aunt Rita's "little girl." Michael Leo and I have always been close, even though he would terrorize me with his pranks and he threw all my dolls into the fireplace! I never did get a replacement for the baby doll he burned.

Uncle Leo was drafted in 1950 and served in the Army during the Korean War in the 7th Cavalry Regiment. He was what the Army called an engineer. His job was to lead the tanks and search and disarm the land mines. On October 3, 1951 while he and the other engineer, Melvin Shields, were on top of the lead tank, they spotted two mines up ahead.

The tanks halted and they went into enemy territory alone to disarm the mines. While they were disarming the mine it exploded and it blew them in different directions; they found themselves surrounded by enemy fire, and were only able to make a break when our friendly artillery fired back at the enemy.

That battle earned my Uncle Leo a Silver Star, the Combat Infantry Badge, the ROK Presidential Unit Citation, the Distinguished Unit Citation, the Korean Service Medal with 3 Bronze Stars and the permanent loss of his hearing. I am proud to say that my Uncle Leo is a Korean War hero.

One of Uncle Leo's favorite meals is stuffed peppers. Now there are many rec-ipes for stuffed peppers, most are stuffed with ground meat and rice; however in my family the recipe is meatless. Since I tend to make the family recipes without regard to measurements and with the ingredients that I have on hand, I decided to make stuffed peppers for our supper to have the recipe to share with you. My mother tells me that my Grandmother would serve the peppers with spaghetti, using the sauce from the peppers. The ingredients used can be substituted with any kind of cheese, like ricotta, blue cheese, mozzarella, but always with grated Romano or Parmigiano cheese.

Chapter 13 photos

Photo #65. Short Leo Bevelaqua and his tall lean top-of-tank companion Melvin Schields a few days prior to October 3, 1951. That was his last day of combat. (Photo from Bevelaqua file)

An article about Uncle Leo being a war hero.

*Service men - **Right:** Uncle Joe in WW II. **Below:** Uncle Mike and Uncle Leo during the Korean War*

Stuffed Peppers

Sauce:
1 tablespoon virgin olive oil
1 small onion, diced
2 cloves garlic, minced
4 fresh basil leaves, chopped
Red pepper to taste
1 can (14.5 oz.) diced tomatoes (pureed)
½ cup red wine

Stuffing for Peppers:
4 peppers, red, green, yellow or orange sliced in half
½ cup plain bread crumbs
½ cup grated Pecorino Romano cheese
½ crumbled goat cheese
3 to 4 chopped Portobello mushrooms
½ chopped black olives
3 tablespoons fresh parsley leaves, chopped
1 tablespoon fresh thyme
1 to 2 eggs, beaten

Heat olive oil in pan large enough to hold the peppers, add onion and cook until translucent, add garlic, basil and red pepper and cook until garlic is golden.

Add the tomatoes and red wine, cook over low heat. Cut peppers in half, clean out seeds. Mix all the other ingredients together, adding enough egg to hold the stuffing together.

Stuff each pepper half full and place them into the pan, spoon sauce over them, cover the pan and cook over very low heat until the peppers are tender. I cooked mine for about 40 minutes. Green peppers take a little longer to cook then the other peppers.

August 2012

Last month we hosted the Lombardi Family Reunion and during the planning stage the subject of lasagna came up. As many of my readers might know, when I first met my husband, Sal he was an undercover detective. He was on loan to the Pawtucket Police Special Squad and I believe that his name at the time was Andy. The year was 1977 and the special squad was where Sal honed his skills as an undercover operative. The guys in the squad were a tight knit group of police detectives, with expertise in organized crime, drugs, street gangs, prostitution, gambling, stolen cars and gypsies. They were all friends and they shared their vast knowledge with Sal.

1981 - My handsome husband Sal in his officers uniform

The Pawtucket Special Squad also had a vast network of law enforcement agency contacts, throughout New England including the federal agencies. Every year the special squad would host a Christmas Party but only for law enforcement. Sal, who had been bragging about his girlfriend's great lasagna, offered that I would make one for the party. So I made an extra-large lasagna for the party and prepared to drive it the mile and a half to the police station. At that time, I was driving a 1968 T-Bird, dark blue four door sedan with leather seats and suicide doors. Just picture me with this large roaster size pan, trying to wrestle it onto the floor in the back seat. Well there was no way I could get it onto the floor, so I decided it would be safe enough on the back seat for the short ride to the station. What could happen?

What happened is the following sad story of that lasagna's demise. I left the apartment and managed to get a few blocks, when suddenly the car in front of me stopped short, I slammed on power brakes to avoid an accident and the lasagna pan went flying off the back seat, flipped over and the lasagna landed on the floor.

I went back to our apartment and called the squad room (this was before cell phones) crying that the lasagna was ruined. Sal was not pleased with me to say the least; he knew he would be in for a lot of ribbing for months to come. The other guys were more understanding to my plight and told me not to worry.

I remember kneeling by the back seat and spooning lasagna from the floor with tears running down by face. I redeemed my reputation at the next special squad party when I once again made them lasagna. It was months before the T-Bird, after many washings, stopped smelling like lasagna. There are many different ways to make lasagna, using different ingredients, sauces and cheeses. Here is the recipe that is traditional for my family.

First I make the gravy, with meatballs and sausage. Remember my definition of gravy is a meat based sauce, which uses a thickener. Brown 1 lb. of sausage, a piece of pork and beef with a little olive oil, deglaze the pan with wine, add the tomatoes, cook until the tomatoes start to change color, then add the tomato paste and slow cook for a couple of hours. (see recipe - September 2006)

After adding the paste, add the meatballs to the gravy. Meatballs are made with ground meat (combination of beef, pork, and veal) breadcrumbs, parsley, Parmesan and/or Romano cheese, pepper and eggs; mixed together; formed into balls and par cooked on a cookie sheet in 375° oven until brown on both sides. Finish cooking the meatballs in the gravy, which adds flavor to the gravy and to the meatballs.

2012 - Costume contest for Clad-in

Lasagna

1 lb. lasagna noodles
3 to 4 cups of gravy or sauce
1 lb. of Ricotta cheese, mixed with 1 beaten egg and about 1 scoop of the gravy
3 hard-boiled eggs, minced
½ cup Parmesan cheese, grated
¾ lb. grated mozzarella cheese
1 lb. of meatballs (after they are cooked in the gravy, remove and either crumble or slice thin) (See April 2012)
1 lb. sausage, sliced or crumbled
1 teaspoon salt
2 tablespoons olive oil

Preheat oven to 350° Bring 5 quarts of water to a boil. Add a heaping teaspoon salt and 2 tablespoons olive oil. Put the lasagna noodles into the boiling water a few at a time, cook about 2 to 3 minutes and remove them with a slotted spoon and put them into a bowl of cold water to stop the cooking. Remove the noodles and lay them in a single layer on a dampened kitchen towel, cover with another dampened towel until ready to assemble the lasagna. Have all your ingredients lined up to assemble the layers.

In a 13" x 9" pan, add enough gravy to cover the bottom, add a layer of the noodles, overlapping them slightly. Dot with the ricotta cheese mixture and spread over the noodles; add some of the meatball and sausage, sprinkle with eggs, mozzarella and Parmesan cheeses and enough gravy to wet the ingredients.

Repeat until the ingredients are used, ending with the last layer of just noodle. Spread the top with gravy, mozzarella and Parmesan cheeses. Bake about 45 minutes or until browned and bubbly. Let rest for about 15 minutes before serving to let the lasagna set.

The deeper the pan you use the better for thicker layers, and you can eliminate the hard-boiled eggs and sausage for a plainer version. I usually make it the day before and reheat it for the lasagna to really set. The slices cut cleaner and are easier to serve. Just remember when transporting lasagna never put it on the back seat and stop short!

September 2012

August was a busy month; it started with the first of five weddings, a car tour on the Connecticut River and a visit with friends in Pennsylvania. The "Woodies on the River" tour started with a drive in the 1941 Cadillac to Essex Connecticut, a stay at the Griswold Inn, a wonderful meals with great friends, a tour of the Connecticut River Museum, watching Carousel at the Goodspeed Opera House, and a visit to Gillette Castle. Our friends Ned and Jan Preli planned the tour for our club and did a wonderful job. It was a great time and it presents a challenge for us since we are planning next year's 20th Anniversary tour.

Sal and I returned from the tour and immediately started to pack for our Pennsylvania visit with Bill and Paulette Mack. Bill was the chief of police in Scituate before retiring and moving to a rural community near Erie, Pennsylvania. Bill and my husband were on the Woonsocket Police Department together and they share a love for antique cars. I would see Bill, Paulette and their daughter, Kelly, on the antique car show circuit during the years and we would chat. At most, we were acquaintances who shared common interests; however, that all changed when Bill was hired as the police chief and they decided to move from Woonsocket to Scituate.

Remembering how hectic it was moving, I had packed a picnic basket with food and welcomed them to Scituate with supper on their first night in town. That was the start of the change from being acquaintances to becoming friends. Food has always played an integral part in our lives, so bringing someone a meal is just a natural event for me. I remember as a kid, when someone new moved into the neighborhood, my mother would bake a cake and bring it to the neighbor to welcome them. So knowing that Bill has a sweet tooth, I decided to bring him his favorite treat as a thank you for the invitation to visit.

I hope you enjoy my Crème De Menthe Brownies recipe.

Crème De Menthe Brownies

1 cup vegetable oil
⅔ cup cocoa
2 cups sugar
½ teaspoon baking powder
2 teaspoons vanilla
½ teaspoon salt
4 eggs
1 cup unsifted flour

Blend oil, sugar, and vanilla in bowl. Add eggs one at a time, beat well with spoon. Combine flour, cocoa, baking powder, salt, and add gradually to mixture until blended. Spread in a greased 15"x10" jelly roll pan. Bake at 350° oven for 15 to 20 minutes or until brownie pull away from pan. Cool

Middle Layer

3 cups sifted confectioners' sugar
1 ½ sticks melted margarine
2 tablespoons green crème de menthe

Mix the ingredients together and spread over brownie layer and let it set.

Last Layer

1 ½ cups melted chocolate chips
½ cup melted margarine

Mix together and pour evenly over middle layer, set overnight. Cut into squares.

October 2012

I have to tell you, retirement is a real change in lifestyle! I have discovered that I have more "free" time but accomplish less, and that breakfast in the morning sunshine with Sal and our cats is one of my favorite pastimes. But nothing can beat having the time to spend with my mother! I am so very lucky to have such a remarkable woman for a mother.

In January, Mary Bevelaqua Grossi will be 99 years old, and she still lives in her own apartment, cooks, bakes, and sews. Last month I took her shopping for clothes, since her great grandson Steven's wedding was in September and her granddaughter Gina is to be married in December, her wardrobe needed to be replenished. What a great day it was!

We shoped and had lunch and, most important of all, she shared stories of her life. We were listening to Forties music, when she told me that she danced to Benny Goodman's Band. She told me that the big bands used to play at Rhodes on the Pawtuxet during its heyday. We had the time to reminisce while driving to and from appointments.

Before Mother's Day, she decided that she would like to experience a facial. So after speaking to my brother and sister, we decided it would be a great gift to treat her to a facial. Now that turned out to be easier said than done, since I needed a spa that was handicap accessible and I wanted to make sure they would take good care of her. After a discussion with Enza Slinko, my hairstylist, she offered to bring the facial table down to the first floor, which is handicap accessible. Valentina even came in on Memorial Day so my mother could have privacy. So for her first facial, my mother was treated like a "Queen."

Later that day, while she was waiting at the Stop and Shop pharmacy for me to shop for her groceries, I found her in conversation with an elderly gentleman. He was quite talkative and it was difficult to drag her away from him. She told me that he wanted to bet her a dollar that she couldn't guess his age. She responded she bet that he couldn't guess her age. He turned out to be 92 years old, and he guessed that she was 76 years old. She does look like she is in her seventies.

On the down side of retirement is the fact that I am spending more time in the kitchen; now I have to make breakfast, lunch and supper. Since Sal likes (and is used to) variety in his meals, I really have to get creative not to make the same dishes. Last week I looked in my refrigerator for inspiration and found Portobello mushroom caps, arugula, a tomato and cheese. What follows is the recipe for my spur of the moment grilled mushrooms.

Micheline's Grilled Portabello Mushrooms

4 large mushroom caps, stems removed
4 slices of tomato
4 handfuls of arugula
4 slices of provolone cheese
Olive oil

Heat the grill to a medium/high heat. Rub olive oil (I used garlic infused oil) on the mushrooms; grill the mushrooms gill side up for about five minutes.

Remove from the grill, and place a handful of the arugula on the mushroom, follow with a slice of tomato and end with a slice of cheese.

Put the mushroom back on the grill and cook until mushroom is cooked and the cheese is melted. This should only take about five minutes.

Sal - photo by Gene Hutnak Photography

November 2012

I always think of November as the jump start of the holiday season and a time for reflection. Thanksgiving always makes me acknowledge the blessings in my life. I am blessed to have found just the right man to share that life, a man of honor and integrity, who is the love of my life. I am blessed to have a wonderful family to share my life. I am blessed to have had my grandmother in my life for 35 years. Most of all, I am thankful for the wonderful memories of shared holidays with my parents, siblings, grandparents, aunts, uncles, cousins and friends.

When I was growing up, my family celebrated Thanksgiving with an Italian twist. The meal would start off with an antipasto made with prosciutto, provolone cheese, salami, olives, and roasted peppers just to name of few of the items on this large platter. Then we would have chicken escarole soup with tiny meatballs served with grated cheese. This is the soup that today is called Italian wedding soup, not that we ever called it by that name! The next course served was lasagna, with meatballs and sausage. What followed was the turkey, with all of the various accompaniments of the traditional American Thanksgiving dinner. The salad was always served during this course. There was always my grandfather's homemade wine served with the meal.

We would rest a little while as the table was cleared of the dinner dishes and room was made for the coffee and dessert. An array of pies, cookies, fresh fruit and roasted chestnuts would be brought to the table with the coffee, espresso and anisette. Of course, there was always mixed nuts and figs, just in case you wanted to pick. I don't know how we managed to eat dessert after all the other food, but we did!

My mom.

Mincemeat-Pear Pie

Piecrust for single 9-inch pie
1 large lemon
3 large fresh pears
1 jar (1 lb., 12 oz.) prepared mincemeat
¾ cup sifted flour
¼ cup sugar
½ teaspoon pumpkin pie spice
¼ cup butter
1 tablespoon of brandy

Bake at 400° for 45 minutes. Makes one 9-inch pie. Make piecrust and fit it into the pie plate, with the overhanging crust fluted to make a stand up edge. Grate 1 teaspoon lemon peel; reserve. Squeeze lemon; measure 2 tablespoons juice; reserve. Pare pears, quarter and core. Slice 1 of the pears into wedges in a small bowl and sprinkle lemon juice over the top and toss to coat well. (This is to keep the pear's color.)

Chop remaining pears finely and mix with lemon peel, brandy, mincemeat and ¼ cup flour. Spoon mixture into prepared pie shell and arrange the pear wedges on top in a pinwheel fashion. Combine the remaining ½ flour, sugar, and pumpkin-pie spice in a small bowl.

Cut in butter with a pastry blender (or two knives) until the mixture is crumbly. Sprinkle crumbs over the top of the pie. Bake until crumbs are golden brown and filling is bubbly. Cool the pie completely.

My mother would always garnish the pie with a lemon rose in the center of the pear pinwheel. To make the lemon rose, start at the stem end and pare off the peel in one continuous long strip. Rewind the spiral, following the natural curl, stand on the stem end and curl the spiral as tightly as you can to resemble an opened rose.

December 2012

Today I looked at the calendar and realized that in a few short weeks, we will be attending my niece, Gina Grossi's, wedding. Since we have just celebrated our 33rd wedding anniversary, it started me thinking about marriage, relationships, and the changes that are made throughout the years. Since this is a column about food, cooking and life, little vignettes of kitchen stories crossed my mind.

I remember cooking at a childhood acquaintance's apartment. She and her husband were newlyweds at the time. She had lived with her parents and grandmother before her wedding so she had minimal opportunity to cook at home. So like many new brides, she learned to cook after her marriage.

Anyway, there I was helping her to prepare a meal and I asked her for a wooden spoon, which to my surprise was missing from her kitchen. I commented "What do you mean; you don't have a wooden spoon! Every kitchen needs wooden spoons, how can you stir anything?" Needless to say, I bought her some wooden spoons.

After that experience, I often made up a "kitchen essential basket," complete with a basic cookbook for many a bridal shower gift. Really, have you ever seen wooden spoons on a bridal registry list?

When first married, I had a set of stainless steel Farberware pans. At the time they were considered top of the line. Today there are more pots and pans from every popular chef than, as the old saying goes, "than Carter has Liver Pills." (I really never knew what that saying meant; I mean what are liver pills? And why did Carter have them? If anyone knows how that saying came about please tell me?)

Now, I married a rare breed of male: he is a man who loves to shop. Really! He not only buys his own clothes, but mine too. He knows what looks good, what style best becomes the individual, what colors enhance and what colors diminish your appearance. He missed his calling in life -- he should have been a personal shopper. Well one day, a few years back, he was on a mission to replace all my pots and pans. I needed to have the best!

He researched the various brands in today's market and decided that I needed to replace my Farberware with a set of Viking pans (they are 7 layers compared to the standard 3 layers). They are nice pans and having a good quality set of pans does make a difference in preparing the meal.

Consequently, since we no longer have inferior cookware, Sal, on occasion, will surprise me by preparing a meal. Sal doesn't follow a recipe-he creates it! He also tells me that he can cook better than me! Unfortunately, he doesn't rise to the bait when I reply that he can take over all the cooking. So what follows is recipe for one of his creations.

Sal's Clam Pasta Delight

1 9 oz. pkg. of portabella mushroom & cheese tortelloni (cooked al dente)
1 6.5 oz. can chopped clams in clam juice
½ green pepper & ½ red pepper, sliced
1 small yellow onion, diced
1 clove garlic, crushed
Red pepper flakes to taste
Olive oil
Romano cheese

Sauté the peppers, onion and garlic in about ¼ cup of olive oil, add red pepper flakes, cover the pan until the peppers and onions are soften.

Add the clams with their juice and cook just long enough for the clams to warm, add your cooked tortelloni and toss until coated with the sauce, add cheese and serve.

Me and Sal. -photo by Clad-in

January 2013

I've never held the belief that one should make New Year's resolutions; it seems as if you make them only to break them. However, I am going to break my own rule for 2013. I have discovered that while I love being retired, I miss the challenges of my career. Every day was different; there were diverse problems to solve, new people to meet, innovative methods to try, and a sense of accomplishment of a job well done.

Of course, with distance, one tends to forget the frustrations of dealing with difficult staff, court personnel, offenders and victims, and lack of staff and supplies as well as the computers that would freeze at a critical moment and take days to fix! I really can't say that I am bored, but rather I seem to lack focus. When you work, you get up and come home at a certain time, you look into the closet to see what to wear, and there is a routine to your day. Retirement is more fluid; there is no timeframe and, if not today, there is always domani (Italian for tomorrow).

Therefore, I have decided that for the year of 2013, I will get into focus, set an agenda, make lists, check off the lists, complete my cookbook and start a cooking demonstration sideline. In terms of challenges, I am planning to develop new recipes and, more importantly, actually write them down.

Since I cook more by instinct, without using measurements, and by experimentation, it is difficult to share the recipes, when it's all in my head. I also discovered that writing a cookbook requires you to be able to have an actual recipe. I mean, who would have thought a cookbook needs recipes, with ingredients, measurements and a serving size!

When I look for a recipe in my numerous cookbooks, I use it for a guide to create the dish, not as a blueprint to make the dish. I now realize that my way is the exception and most people follow the directions. So with that in mind, I will now measure, mark down and try to be precise in my directions when I create a new dish.

I have decided to share a recipe for a cheese ball that I developed without nuts. I realized that more often than not most cheese balls either have nuts in them or are rolled in them. So here is my recipe for a cheese ball without nuts.

Gorgonzola & Cranberry Cheese Ball

8 oz. Cream cheese
3 oz. Gorgonzola cheese, crumble (you can use any blue cheese)
2 tablespoons chopped celery
1 tablespoon minced onion
Few drops of Tabasco® sauce
Dash of cayenne pepper
¾ cup chopped dried cranberries

Combine cheeses. Blend in next 4 ingredients.
Chill for an hour. Then shape into ball or log.
Roll in chopped cranberries to cover, chill.
Serve the cheese ball at room temperature.

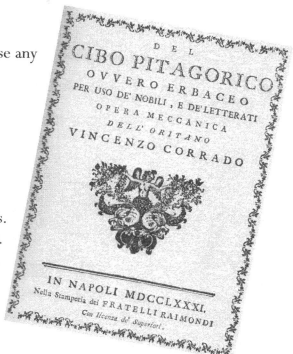

Add your own twist...

February 2013

On January 15th, my mother turned 99 years young. She had expressed to her children that she did not want a party this year. So in accordance with her wishes, we decided not to give her a party. My mother lives in senior housing and is a member of the Scituate Vista Association. Barbara and Adele, two women from the complex, had other ideas! They decided that Mary's 99th birthday just had to be celebrated. Since they didn't want to surprise her, they told her it was going to be a small affair, held in the community room at the complex. Adele contacted me to ask if I would invite some of the family.

Well some of the family turned out to be her two sisters, Helen and Tessie; her brother Leo; her sister-in-law, Arline; her cousin, Netta; her nephew, Johnny; my brother, Joe, with his two daughters, Gina and Brianna; my niece Tanya; her husband, Delbert; her sons, Steven, DJ, James; her daughter-in-law, Kathryn; her grandson, Simon; and Sal and me.

There would have been more, but my sister, her other two daughters, grandchildren and great granddaughter are currently in Utah. That would have been a small affair, but Barbara and Adele posted a notice about the party on the bulletin board and in the elevators. When my mother found out about the notice, she went into panic mode about her hair, she needed a haircut. Now it's not always easy to get an appointment on short notice with a good hair stylist and I needed one before the week was out since the party was on Sunday.

When I called my hair stylist, Enza, bless her wonderful heart, she made room for my mother between her appointments on that Saturday to make sure my mother looked her best. On Saturday, I picked her up and treated her to a day of beauty and lunch. She reminded me that Saturday was also my father's birthday and, had he lived, he would have been 102 years old (he was 75 when he died in 1986).

It was a great day, made better because my mother had baked the day before and she had made white wine biscuits (a personal favorite) which I shared with Enza, her staff and customers. Little did we know, but Barbara had called the *Cranston Herald* and there was a photographer there to take her picture. The party was wonderful, so many of her friends in the complex came to celebrate her longevity.

I thought I would share one of my father's favorite recipes for custard pie. My mother told me that a baker friend of my father had shared the recipe with him.

Custard Pie

One 10" unbaked pie crust
6 eggs
1 cup of sugar
½ teaspoon salt
¼ teaspoons ground nutmeg
2 tablespoon flour (secret ingredient)
1 quart whole milk (she has also made the pie with 1% milk)

Preheat oven to 450° Beat the eggs, sugar, salt and flour until mixed, add the milk and nutmeg. Pour into 10" unbaked pie crust. Bake for 15 minutes, then lower oven to 375° and cook about 25 to 30 minutes until the center is set. The pie is done when a knife cut in the center of the pie comes out clean.

The family at Mom's 99th birthday party.

March 2013

Last month Sal and I happened to catch an episode of *Hawaii Five-O* on television. It was the episode that featured a murderer who was killing police officers. It was based on the original 1973 *Hawaii Five-O* episode called "Hook Man" that featured a double amputee as the murderer. I remember watching the original show with my father, and being amazed at what the man accomplished with his hooks. Unlike the recent episode, the original show featured J. J. Armes, a double amputee, who was a private investigator in real life. It was of special interest to us because my father was an amputee.

In February of 1955, when I was four years-old, my father was in an industrial accident that resulted in having his left arm amputated just below the elbow. He was 44 years-old at the time. He truly was an amazing man; he never considered himself disabled. He used a working man's hook that allowed him to be a welder on submarines; paint and hang wallpaper; do mechanic work on our cars and he could tie his shoelaces with one hand. My father also had a prosthetic hand, which looked real, but did not have the capabilities of his hook. The hand was covered by a lifelike glove, which would sometimes rip, so Dad would cover the rip with a band aide.

One day a friend had come to ask my father to "lend him a hand" on some project. My father whispered to me to go upstairs and get his hand out of the bureau drawer, which he then offered to his friend. I can still see the look on that man's face! My father was so capable that people forgot he was an amputee. He often made me his accomplice in his tricks.

For instance, he would place a dollar bill in his hook and then offer the dollar to some child with the caveat that it was theirs if they could remove it without it tearing. No matter how hard they tried, they never could retrieve the dollar. Then I, little Miss Innocent, would pluck the dollar right out of the hook, with just a little release of pressure from Dad!

Whenever children saw him, they would point and whisper to their parents, "look, there's Captain Hook." He never tried to scare them and often would show them how the hook operated. Since, I never thought of my father as different, I never mentioned to new friends that he was an amputee. So when a new boy came to pick me up for a date, and my father didn't like his looks, he would greet him by reaching out with his left hook instead of his right hand. You can imagine the effect it had on the guy! So for this trip down memory lane, I am going to share a recipe for one of Dad's favorite cookies. They are called "Thief Boys" and they are so good you just have to steal them as soon as they are baked.

Thief Boys

1 ½ pkg. yeast
1 teaspoon sugar
¼ cup warm water
1 ½ cup butter
2 ⅓ cup sugar
¾ cup hot milk
5 cups flour
3 eggs, beaten
1 ½ cups finely chopped walnuts or pecans

Preheat oven to 350° Mix yeast, sugar and warm water together. Combine ½ cup butter and ½ cup sugar add hot milk and stir until butter is melted. Combine with the yeast mixture. Add in 2 cups flour and beat until smooth; then beat in eggs, adding remaining flour to make a soft dough.

Place in greased bowl, turning to grease the top. Cover and let rise in a warm place until doubled in bulk, about 1 hour. Divide dough into fourths. Shape each fourth into 12 inch rolls. Divide each roll into 12 pieces, and shape each piece into a 7 inch rope.

Dip each into melted butter, then sugar, then butter, then chopped nuts. Fold each rope into half; twist to make a braid.

Place on greased baking sheet and cover. Let rise until double, about 20 minutes. Bake for 15-20 minutes. This recipe makes about 4 dozen cookies.

April 2013

Having worked in the criminal justice field and being married to a law enforcement officer for nigh on 34 years, I have developed a slightly different way of looking at the world. I am a skeptic when it comes to technological advances, leery of using them and all too aware of the many misapplications of their uses. So it really came as a surprise to me that I have actually found Facebook to be useful and enjoyable. For many years I successfully resisted being on Facebook; in fact, doing so only because my wonderful clerical staff convinced me to try it out. I am thankful that they introduced me to its advantages as I have been able to share in their lives albeit remotely. It is a great tool to keep in touch with friends and family, advertise your business and to discover people who have temporarily slipped off your personal radar.

A few months ago, I discovered an acquaintance on Facebook, who was very important in our life. In the late 1980's, Sal decided to become a Big Brother, and as a result a 13 year-old boy named Mario came into our life. When Sal first met Mario, he was living with his maternal grandmother and his older brother in the Hartford projects; not a great place, to say the least. Sal was able to demonstrate to his grandmother that she could afford to move out of the projects and return to her roots to live on Federal Hill. I, in turn, made sure she was provided with the social services necessary to assist the elderly.

Mario became a member of our family; we introduced him to family and friends; brought him to antique car shows; showed him a better life and, of course, cooked him meals. I am so proud of his accomplishments: he completed school, is a caring and supportive father and husband and, a successful salesman. Mario married a wonderful woman named Grace and has two children, his daughter, Bella (17), and his son, Sammy (14).

Mario and his family moved out of Rhode Island when his children were very young. In fact, Bella was only two the last time they visited us. Then I discovered Mario on Facebook and we reconnected. It seemed as though fate had a hand in bringing us together as it just so happens that on our upcoming travels we will be in their neighborhood. What a wonderful visit. Grace cooked a delicious meal and we caught up on each other's lives.

It's funny how Mario married a girl who has traits and interests similar to mine. She is a great cook, family orientated, and has a career that parallels my own. So while the guys caught up with their lives, we talked about her work and recipes. Since Mario likes butternut squash and Grace likes beans, I told her that I would send her my recipe for, what else, Italian squash and beans.

Traditionally my mother would make this dish with Hubbard squash, which is available in late spring, but it's difficult to find even then, and it is a large squash. So I substitute butternut instead.

Italian Squash & Beans

1 small onion, diced
2 cups butternut squash, diced into bite size pieces
1 small carrot, shredded
1 lb. of cooked or canned (16 oz.) beans (cannelloni or navy beans)
2 cloves garlic, crushed
1 can (14.5 oz.) diced tomatoes (fire roasted, spicy red pepper), pureed
1 tablespoon fennel seed
½ cup of red wine or water if necessary
Red pepper flakes to taste

Sauté the onions, carrots and red pepper flakes in virgin olive oil until transparent, add the squash and fennel seed and cook until the squash softens, add garlic and cook until garlic is golden in color.

Add the tomatoes and wine and cook until squash and tomatoes are done. The tomatoes should darken in color and squash should be tender, but not mush.

Lastly, add the beans and cook until they are heated through; add more wine or water if the sauce is too thick and season to taste.

1996 - Sal's "little brother" Mario Belluscio and his daughter Isabella.

May 2013

During my 36 year relationship with my husband, I have been introduced to and infused with the antique car world. Growing up I had no clue that there were cars named Packard, Hudson, Pierce Arrows, Kaisers, LaSalle as well as Cadillac, Lincoln, Oldsmobile and Chevy. When I met Sal, he was driving a 1947 Packard Clipper; what a way to impress a girl!

During the years that followed, we have owned many different vehicles, several different models of Packard, Cadillac, Buick and even a Hudson! Currently we own a 1941 Cadillac 60 Special that has wood trim. We also belong to the Yankee Wood Chapter of the National Woodie Club. In fact, Sal is the President and I am the Secretary of the chapter. It is a wonderful club, as it is more a couples' social club than a "car club."

This year is the 20th anniversary of the founding of the chapter, so to celebrate I planned a tour in April. We had decided to tour the Newport area and I was looking for either B&B's or inns that are reasonable in price and, most importantly, have parking lots to accommodate the antique cars. The restaurants also have to have parking lots, not an easy feat in Newport. On top of lodging and meals, you also needed activities and scheduled free time.

So in January, the word went out to the club requesting their interest and, more importantly, their commitment to participate. Armed with that knowledge, Sal and I set out to find the lodging location.

We found the perfect spot! It was a beautiful six bedroom B&B, The Villa One Twenty, and a 23 room inn, The Carriage House Inn, which are directly across the street from each other in Middletown. Four couples stayed at the Villa One Twenty and three couples stayed at the Carriage House Inn, with our meeting place being the Villa.

Now, it has historically rained on all of our tours, and this year was no different, with the dreary forecast, much to our disappointment, a decision was made to go "modern," sans the antique cars. Most arrived on Thursday, having travelled from Connecticut, Massachusetts, and Rhode Island, so it was an early dinner at The Atlantic Beach Club. On Friday, in the rain, we traveled to Little Compton to view a private car collection, then a stop at the Sakonnet Winery (before a roaring fire so we could dry out) for a tasting, and on to lunch at The Boat House in Tiverton.

Saturday morning we held our annual meeting and gift swap in The Villa One Twenty's dining room, where we were served coffee and assorted breakfast pastry on an antique table with china dishes. The Villa One Twenty is elegant, decorated with style and class, and is a warm and welcoming establishment, minutes from Newport.

Later that day, it was on to tour Rough Point, Doris Duke's summer mansion. It was an hour and a half tour, that was informative and the artwork and furnishings were exquisite. Well worth the time.

We met that evening at the Newport Playhouse & Cabaret, where we feasted on a diverse and tasty buffet; saw an excellent comedy; and topped the night off with a hilarious cabaret. I have to say, whether it rains or the sun shines, the YWC gang always has a good time.

You might be asking what recipe could possibly tie in with this story. Well one of the restaurant items on the menu was for fried risotto balls, Arancini di Riso, which I made for the first time with friends while on vacation.

1982 - Me and a 1937 Cadillac at a Father's Day car show at Portsmouth Abby

Above: The 1954 Buick Skylark
Below: The Villa One Twenty, off Main Street in Newport, RI. www.VillaOneTwenty.com

Arancini di Riso "Stuffed Risotto Balls"

1 cup bread crumbs, seasoned, set aside in a medium bowl

Filling:
2 cups cooked and cooled risotto
½ cup bread crumbs, seasoned with parsley, basil, pepper
½ cup finely grated Parmesan
¼ cup finely chopped fresh basil leaves
2 eggs, at room temperature, beaten
4 oz. Gorgonzola, at room temperature, cut into 16 (½-inch) cubes

In a medium bowl, combine the risotto, bread crumbs, Parmesan, basil, and beaten eggs. With damp hands, using about 2 tablespoons of the risotto mixture, form the mixture into 1 ¾-inch diameter balls. Make a hole in the center of each ball and insert one of the cubes of Gorgonzola cheese. Cover the hole completely to enclose the cheese.

Roll the balls into the bread crumbs to coat. In a large heavy-bottomed saucepan, pour in enough oil to fill the pan about ⅓ of the way. Heat over medium heat until a thermometer inserted reaches 350° (hint: without a thermometer, a cube of bread will brown in about 2 minutes). Fry the risotto balls in batches, turning occasionally, until golden, about 5 to 6 minutes. Drain on paper towels and serve warm., with a tomato sauce. I had used left over spinach risotto, but you can use any kind and add prosciutto, ham, and any kind of cheese you like for variety. It a great way to use that left over risotto.

June 2013

In the mid 1960's, my mother's family decided that we needed to have a family reunion. The reunion would encompass the members of the Bevelaqua and Iantosco families. My Great Grandmother, Antoinetta Iantosco, had three children; Uncle Mike, Uncle Leo, and my Grandmother, Michelina. Uncle Mike and Aunt Fanny had three children, Uncle Leo and Aunt Frances had two children, and my Grandmother and Grandfather had 8 children; who all had children, some of whom had children of their own.

So you can see this was no small event; it was a major undertaking! All of the aunts and married cousins would meet once a month for coffee and dessert, to organize the reunions. The meetings served a dual purpose; it was a social gathering that kept the family close and, of course, they were the planning sessions for the event. All the women paid dues that went toward the expense of the affair and they met at different homes each month. On occasion I accompanied my mother, and I remember one October meeting where they dressed in costume and partied while planning. Seeing my mother dressed as a little girl, wearing a yellow yarn pigtail wig and riding a tricycle is a sight I will never forget.

I called my Aunt Tessie to reminisce and add some details to family planning sessions. She remembered that the meetings were held on a night that she would miss her favorite TV show, which my mother said was Peyton Place. We held the reunions at the Club 400 (where the West Valley Inn is located now). It was a great place, because we would go into the restaurant for a sit-down dinner and then go across the parking lot to the field to play games and later we would have hamburgers and hot dogs. There was only one hall back in the day and the rest of the land was large enough to play baseball. Best of all it was private!

We would have three-legged races, toss eggs (raw) to each other widening the distance with each toss, and pass the orange from chin to chin. There were games for the kids and for the adults. It was great fun. The reunions continued on a yearly basis until the early 1970's. This summer, some of my cousins have arranged another reunion, and in this day of social media they have turned to Facebook to spread the word. I'm not sure how this will work as not all the family has a computer or, if they do; are they on Facebook?

I guess I'm just an old-fashioned kind of gal, but I prefer the face to face social interactions when planning events. Not to mention that it's nice to visit with the family.

Since there is no rain date and it has been planned to be outdoors, I guess we have to hang the rosary beads on the clothes line overnight to ask for fair weather. Does anyone still have a clothes line? I have a great recipe for pickled eggplant to take as a side dish to a picnic. It's good because it does not need to be kept refrigerated during the picnic.

Above: *May 1944 - Uncle Leo, a golden gloves champ & Uncle Mikey wearing his WWII Army cadet uniform in Providence.*

Me, Tanya, Jade and Iswzabella. - Photo by Kayla Salony Photography.

Melanzane Sott'Aceto "Pickled Eggplant"

1 small eggplant
½ cup white balsamic vinegar
1 tablespoon capers, rinsed
½ red, yellow, orange pepper, sliced into thin strips
1 tablespoon chopped fresh parsley
1 teaspoon chopped fresh basil
¼ cup virgin olive oil

Peel eggplant, slice in half, then into thin slices, turn the eggplant and slice into thin match like sticks. Place eggplant in a strainer, salt, and place a plate over it with a weigh on top of it (a can of tomatoes works great).

Let stand for about 1 hour. Rinse and pat the eggplant dry. Place in a bowl with the remaining ingredients and mix well.

Refrigerate overnight and it's ready to serve, either cold or room temperature.

July 2013

During the 1950's, my family lived in an extended household on Borden Street, which is one street away from Rhode Island Hospital. On top of that, all my aunts and uncles lived within walking distance from our house. In those days the neighborhood was primarily Irish and Italian, but by the late 1950's the cultural dynamics changed and family all relocated to the suburbs, except for us, we moved to the Mt. Pleasant area. As a young girl, I remember going downtown with my mother and always sharing a coffee cabinet at the Outlet Company or riding the bus with my Aunt Rita. As I said, aunts, uncles and cousins were always nearby in the neighborhood.

There is a story told in my family about my running away from home when I was four years-old. I left the house one summer day along with my dog, Army, without my grandparents' knowledge. Either that, or I told them I was running away from home. I have always asserted that I was not running away, but I was going to go visit my Aunt Helen and Uncle Joe, who lived on Chester Avenue. Anyway, I set off on my adventure early that day wandering around looking for my aunt's house. I think that I went left instead of right and never found the house. My mother tells me that I went in the opposite direction and walked to Haywood Park and ended up close to downtown near the Providence Public Library.

Well by the afternoon, I was quite lost and very thirsty, so I went to a house to ask for a drink of water. A nice woman took me in to give me a drink. She quickly ascertained that I was lost and called the local police station. Meanwhile back at home, the search had begun looking for the little runaway. I'm not quite sure how I managed to walk so far from home, but I landed at a police station a distance away. Back in those days it wasn't standard procedure to teach a child their address, so the police had no clue where I came from.

Somehow or other, the family did find me and my father came to retrieve me. I remember riding a tricycle, drinking hot chocolate and eating cookies at the station. I was having a great time; who wanted to go home with such attention?

To this day, the family still thinks that I ran away. My father said that Army was very protective and wouldn't let anyone near me. I have to admit that when I was a little older I would threaten to run away, but I always came back! So in honor of the Providence Police officers who braved my dog's protective stance to feed me cookies, it is only fitting to share a cookie recipe this month.

Cranberry-White Chocolate Chip Cookies

½ cup butter, softened
⅔ cup sugar
1 large egg, slightly beaten
1 teaspoon ground cinnamon
1 cup all-purpose flour
1 ⅓ cups old-fashioned oatmeal
1 teaspoon baking soda
1 cup dried cranberries
½ cup white chocolate chips

Preheat oven to 350° In large bowl, beat together butter, sugar and egg until smooth and creamy. In separate bowl, mix together cinnamon, flour, oatmeal and baking soda until well-combined.

Gradually add dry mixture to the butter mixture until it is all mixed; then stir in dried cranberries and chocolate chips until blended. Drop dough by rounded teaspoons onto cookie sheets coated with cooking spray, bake for 10 to 12 minutes. This recipe makes about 3 dozen cookies.

November 1945 - My Aunt Helen & Uncle Joe Badessa on their wedding day in Providence. photograph by Ansaldi Photography.

August 2013

This month I am turning 63 years-old (which I figure is middle age since my mother is 99 and longevity runs in my family) and I have come to the realization that some life style changes are in order. Not having to get up every morning, checking out the weather to decide what to wear, running around to get ready, dealing with rush hour traffic, and then the challenge of a high stress job is wonderful. Having the ability to spend time with my mother is invaluable, as well as spending time with my husband; however, it does have its drawbacks!

It's so easy to fall into a pattern of sleeping late, hanging around the house, watching TV or reading, and not getting anything accomplished. I'm beginning to believe that the more active you are, the younger you feel; you just need the motivation to get going. That, I'm finding, is easier said than done!

I started walking and I was up to about 3 miles a day, then the rains came, and then the heat wave, so I have to start all over again (once I get shoes that I can walk in without my feet hurting. Is that a sign of age?). Of course, being at home most of the time makes food so much more accessible; there's always time for a snack and it's usually not a healthy choice, so now the pounds start to add up.

Well that's what has been happening to me. I found myself in a rut and I was not a happy camper! So I made the decision to lose weight and get back into shape. Once I'm back in fighting shape, I'm going to clean out my closet and give away my business suits and professional wardrobe to my working relatives and the Trinity Thrift Store.

Then, I'm going to go shopping for a whole new look at A Charmed and Dangerous Place in the village and, with a new wardrobe to show off, why would I want to stay at home?! Losing weight is not easy and keeping the weight off means making life-style changes. So I have been experimenting with new dishes that are lower in calories and healthier. I would like to share a recipe for chicken salad that I think is a winner.

Micheline's Chicken Salad

2 cups of cooked diced white chicken
¼ cup diced celery
¼ cup dried cranberries
¼ cup dried blueberries
¼ chopped pecans
2 to 3 tablespoons of plain non-fat Greek yogurt
Black pepper to taste

Makes 4 servings. Mix all ingredients together and add just enough of the yogurt to lightly coat the mixture, serve on lettuce.

The chicken and yogurt are the protein, the berries add fiber and sweetness, and the pecans add healthy oil to your diet.

I'm not a dietitian, but a rough calculation of all the ingredients brings a 1 cup serving to be about 220 calories per serving.

August 1959 - My birthday party

September 2013

August has been a month of dilemmas for me; it seems as if I get one problem solved and another pops up. At the end of July, Sal and I went on a cruise up to Canada and even though it rained most of the week, we still had a wonderful time with a great group of "Fun Seekers."

It was on this cruise, that I discovered cold fruit soups. I tried strawberry, peach, mango, and a cucumber-dill soup. Let me tell you, I fell in love with the fruit soups. I decided to add them to my collection of recipes, starting with the strawberry. I researched the Internet for recipes and found a few that I planned to try, with my final version for this article. Unfortunately, life got in the way and I only tried one recipe, but I wasn't turned on! So, I will keep experimenting and my faithful followers will have to wait just a while longer.

As I said, life interrupted my kitchen plans, with my mother's side trip to the hospital. Thankfully, all the tests were negative and they released her in time for our family reunion. (My sister and I were going to kidnap her, if they didn't release her. She was determined to attend this reunion.) So here it is, the night before the reunion and my birthday, and I have just realized that the deadline for the article is here and I have not perfected my planned recipe.

So on to plan B! Tomorrow, Sal and I are going to pick up my mother in the 1941 Cadillac for the drive to the reunion at Goddard Park. Since she is the oldest member of the family attending, we decided that she should arrive in style. It also happens to be my birthday, so I decided to pack a picnic lunch that is not the usual picnic fare.

First, I made my Italian potato salad, with red, white, and purple potatoes. I also decided to make pickled eggplant, one of my mother's favorite dishes. I'm making enough to share with my Aunt Tessie, since she told me that she hasn't had any in ages. To go with the vegetables, I made a chicken dish with roasted peppers and marinated artichoke hearts. I decided to cheat just a little this time and bought a roasted chicken. You can also cheat by using store- bought roasted peppers. (I did roast my own peppers, as they taste so much better.) This is a quick, but elegant salad that looks like you spent hours preparing.

Chicken Salad with Roasted Peppers & Artichoke Hearts

First, roast 4 or 5 red, yellow, and orange peppers over a grill until the skin blackens on all sides. Place the cooked peppers in a paper bag and seal. The peppers will steam in the bag making it easy to remove the skins.

Once the peppers are cold enough to handle, just peel the skins and remove the seeds. Cut into strips, and add one or two cloves of crushed garlic and virgin olive oil, with a little salt and pepper.

If cheating, remove all the meat from the bones and slice into strips. Or you can grill chicken breasts and slice them.

Arrange the chicken, peppers, and artichoke hearts on the plate and drizzle with an aged balsamic vinegar, and top with finely chopped parsley.

October 2013

As I have mentioned before, I am a member of the Scituate Rotary Club, and this past month we hosted, along with a Massachusetts Rotary Club, an Open World Program Delegation from Russia. The delegation was composed of young professionals from various fields as well as a professional interpreter. The Open World Program is a congressionally sponsored program that brings emerging leaders from Russia, Ukraine, and other Eurasian states to United States. The goal is to give them firsthand exposure to the American system of democracy and free enterprise.

The delegation is housed with Rotary host families and a program of meetings and activities planned around a specific theme. The Open World Program theme for this project was "Accountable Governance" and I was the program coordinator for our portion of the visit. The group began their visit with the Massachusetts Rotary Club on a Friday and had the weekend to socialize before the meetings started. They arrived in Rhode Island on a Tuesday afternoon, with the meetings scheduled the very next morning. I had arranged for meetings with a variety of state, town, and city officials, a tour of the *Providence Journal*, interviews with Leadership RI, and meetings at the Human Rights Commission and the Ethics Commission.

Since I had not met the group, I decided that it just made sense to host a welcoming dinner at my home. I played around with menu ideas for days, "what could I make that would appeal to a group of young Russian men and women?" Finally after much contemplation, I decided to make chicken zingarella, tortellini with grape tomatoes, prosciutto and goat cheese, roasted vegetables, a salad with strawberries and figs and a cold peach and mango soup. (I gave up on the strawberry soup for now.)

They all liked the choices I had prepared and the soup was a great hit! What followed that dinner was a wonderful experience, sharing our ideals, culture, songs and becoming friends. I look forward to our club's hosting another Open World Delegation. When I decided on the cold fruit soup, I looked up several different recipes and then decided to create my own. So I am going to share that recipe this month. The cold soup can be an appetizer or dessert. All I know is there was just about two small bowls left and I made enough for 20 people. I have scaled down the recipe by half.

Peach-Mango Soup

1 lb. frozen peaches
1 lb. frozen mango
1 cup half & half
1 cup Greek vanilla yogurt

⅛ teaspoon each of cinnamon and nutmeg
¼ cup limoncello
1 to 2 tablespoons brown sugar

Puree the peaches and mango, with sugar in a blender. Then blend in the rest of the ingredients until it is well mixed.

If the soup is too thick, add more half & half (or milk) until it is the consistency that you like. Serve the soup cold. I had a bowl of ice and I set the bowl of soup into that bowl to keep it cold.

Halloween 1981 - My niece, Terésa Capobianco.

November 2013

I recently attended a ceremony where I was recognized for my 29-year career in the criminal justice field. Although it was two years after my retirement, it was nice to have my life's work acknowledged. Anyway, it started me thinking about how a nice girl like me ended up with a career in community corrections. It's not like there are any other members of my family in that field, or even in a closely related field, so why work with offenders?

The more I thought about it, the more I realized that my mother influenced me early in my life. She taught me to stand up to bullies, stand up for myself, and stand up for my beliefs. You know how some memories just stand out in your mind, maybe just in the back, just ready to pop out. Well, I remember one instance that pops out in my musings of my career choice. I lived on Borden Street in South Providence until I was seven when we relocated to Mt. Pleasant. When my mother's family first moved to South Providence the neighborhood was primarily Irish and Italian; by the late 50's, the neighborhood changed as the Italians moved to the suburbs and the next minority group replaced the last.

By the time I was four or five, there were only a few white families on the street. I was always allowed to play with the neighborhood kids, whatever their color, as my mother judged people not by the color of their skin, but by their character.

On this one day, I was playing with a little boy and somehow he slapped me. I remember running home and crying to my mother. As she was comforting me, she asked if I had slapped him back. Between tears I said, "No." Well she took me by the hand and we went right over to his house.

By this time, the boy had run to the shelter of his father. My mother yelled up at the window to send down the boy because I was going to confront him. She yelled up that if he didn't come down she was going to go up to the third floor and drag him down by the ear.

Now that boy's father was one big man and my mother is a little bit of nothing, but she showed no fear and, lo and behold, the little boy was suddenly in front of me. My mother instructed me to hit him back and always fight back. From that point on, I always stood up to the bullies. My mother never drove a car, she either used public transportation or she walked everywhere; granted, back in those days, it was a lot safer to walk the city than it is now.

When I started my freshman year at Classical High School, I would take the bus from Academy Avenue to Atwells Avenue and get off at Dean Street and walk to West-minster Street. In the early 1960's Dean Street was a bit shabby, with both the Gemini and Mohegan Hotels (favorites of the streetwalkers) and dive bars lining the street.

Usually it was safe enough to walk in the early morning hours, with just an occasional drunk or flasher making an appearance, but my mother gave me this advice just in case: "when you walk down the street and you see someone that doesn't look quite right, cross to the opposite side of the street; if someone follows you, look for a place with people and go into it (safety in numbers); if all else fails act as if you are crazy and they will leave you alone."

I'm not sure if that advice would work in today's society with all the crazies out there, but it always made me feel a lot safer knowing that I had a plan. She helped mold me into the strong independent woman I am today, one who is comfortable knowing how to handle working in a challenging career with offenders and dealing with the seamier sides of society.

Today, I am going to share my version of a pizza that my Uncle Mike would make every so often.

Caramelized Onion Pizza

1 lb. of pizza dough rolled out onto a peel, spread with corn meal.
(The corn meal will let you slide dough onto the stone when ready to bake)
1 large Spanish onion, sliced

Black olives
Chopped ham (any kind)
Sliced mushrooms
Pepper to taste
About 1/4 cup of crumbled goat cheese

Heat the oven to 450° Slice the onions the width you want them. Use a wide, thick-bottomed sauté pan for maximum pan contact with the onions. Coat the bottom of the pan with 1 teaspoon olive oil, or a mixture of olive oil and butter. Heat the pan on medium high heat until the oil is shimmering.

Add the onion slices and stir to coat the onions with the oil. Spread the onions out evenly over the pan and let cook, stirring occasionally. Depending on how strong your stovetop burner is you may need to reduce the heat to medium or medium low to prevent the onions from burning or drying out.

After 10 minutes, sprinkle some salt over the onions, and if you want, you can add some sugar to help with the caramelizing process. I add a little balsamic vinegar right toward the end of the process. Spread the onions on the pizza dough; add the chopped ham, black olives, and mushrooms. Top with the crumbled goat cheese and bake for about 20 to 25 minutes until the dough is golden brown on the bottom. All ovens cook differently, so you need to check to make sure the dough is not over baked.
Note: *I use a pizza stone, which I place in the cold oven and heat to the 450° temperature.*

December 2013

As I have mentioned, my mother will be 100 years young in January and she is throwing herself a party! She has enlisted me as her event planner, and we have been busy with all the little details. It is a joy to see how excited she is to invite her many friends (a number of them are in their 90's) and her family. It seems that every few days she adds another person to the list. Although I am planning and designing the invitations, she has the final say in all the details. When I suggested purple and white African Violets as the center piece (she always had such beautiful African Violets), she said that was a no go! Instead, she decided to sew a plastic bag holder for each table, which will be added to a basket of goodies made by her daughters and granddaughters, and wrapped beautifully by my friend, Barbara, at Cute as a Button.

This whole process has evoked so many memories of watching my mother sew and bake, and all the good times we had with family and friends. So, it only makes sense to have a basket of goodies that represent her talents and family tradition.

When I designed her "Save the Date" card, I used one of my favorite pictures of her. She is standing on a porch with a lovely coat with fur trim and a beautiful hat, gray with a purple feather, and it was taken in 1942 on her honeymoon. She is just stunning! She still has the hat, which I'm trying to convince her to wear to her party.

In addition to the memories, it has instilled the motivation to complete my cookbook for her birthday. After much thought and consideration, I decided to publish my stories and recipes as I wrote them for the *Foster Home Journal* starting in September 2006 and ending with this last story for December 2013. Of course, that plan might go right out the window depending with how many pages the entire project generates.

I have enlisted my friend and former secretary, Trisha, to do her magic and get all the font, margins and pages just right (God knows I tried and almost gave up on the cookbook); and my friend, Stefanie, and her daughter, Samantha, to design the cover (with the lure of pizza and fudge ribbon cake). So, with some luck, it will be published on her 100th birthday.

My sister, AnneMarie, is helping to edit, and maybe I'll have my great niece, Jade, help with designing some of the chapter dividers. Meanwhile, in the middle of this project, I decided to clean closets, which resulted in turning my whole house upside down, and our Christmas party is just around the corner! So who needs to sleep anyway! I decided to share a recipe that I adapted from an old *Ann Pillsbury's Baking Book,* first published in 1950. (Wait a minute; if the cookbook is old since it was published in 1950, does that make me old too, since I was born the same year?) My mother has used this cook book for years and one day I bought my own copy for 25 cents.

This recipe is a fruit-nut snack bread, which stays moist and fresh for days, and leftovers make a great bread pudding.

Fruit & Nut Bread

¼ cup shortening
2 ½ cups of sifted flour
4 teaspoons baking powder
1 teaspoon salt
1 cup sugar
1 cup of milk
1 egg
½ cup chopped walnuts
½ cup finely chopped apricots
½ cup finely chopped dried cranberries
½ cup finely chopped dried blueberries

Pie Crust Chart

The size of the pan you use for baking a pie is important. Measure the pan across top from outer edge. You can make tarts and pastry strips with the extra pastry, but it is better to use a recipe suited to the pan and the size of the finished pie you want.

Crust Size Chart:	6" Double 8" Single 9" Single	8" Double 9" Double 10" Single	10" Double
Sifted Flour	1 ⅓ cups	2 cups	3 cups
Salt	½ Tsp.	1 Tsp.	1 ½ Tsp.
Crisco®	½ cup	¾ cup	1 cup & 2 Tbsp.
(butter flavor)			
Water (cold)	3 Tbsp.	4 Tbsp.	6 Tbsp.

Combine flour and salt in a bowl. Cut in Crisco® until mixture is uniform and very fine. Sprinkle water over this mixture, a tablespoon at a time, tossing lightly with a fork. Work dough into a firm ball. (Do not over work.) For double crust, divide dough in half for two balls.
(Wrap in waxed paper and refrigerate to let dough rest, while you make the filling. It will make the crust flaky.)

Roll dough about 1/8" thick on a lightly floured surface. Place in pie plate and trim even with the edge of the plate.

Add filling. Roll other half of dough in the same manner and place over the filling.

Trim edges about ½" beyond the edge of the plate. Fold under edge of the bottom crust and flute to seal.

Cut small steam vents in the top crust.

INDEX

Cookies, Cakes, Pies & More, *continued*

Chocolate Speckled Chiffon Cake, 59
Cranberry-White Chocolate Chip Cookies, 199
Crème De Menthe Brownies, 175
Custard Pie, 185
Date Nut Bars, 97
Fudge Ribbon Cake, 13
Italian Almond Cookies, 9
Italian Rice Pie, 17
Kahlua® Liqueur, 153
Micheline's Mexicali Brownies, 99
Mincemeat Foldovers, 95
Mincemeat-Pear Pie, 179
Molasses Sugar Cookies, 149
Pepper Biscuits, 26
Prune Filled Italian Egg Biscuits, 70
Pumpkin Cake, 151
Red & White Wine Biscuits, 27
Ricotta Pie, 17
Sfingi Di San Giuseppe, 79
Sweet & Crunchy Nuts, 121
Sweetened Condensed Milk, 121
Thief Boys, 187
Thumbprint Cookies, 97
Toasted Rosemary Pecans, 121
Wacky Cake, 21
Zabaglione (Dessert Sauce), 157
Zeppoli, 79

Entrées
Baked Peach French Toast, 135
Baked Rigatoni with Sausage, Spinach, Ricotta and Fontina, 85
Chicken Cacciatore, 93
Chicken Cutlet Casserole, 83

Soups

Chicken Escarole Soup with Little Meatballs, 123

Lentils & Rice Soup, 41

Pasta and Beans, 4

Pasta E Fagiole, 5

Patata Zuppa, 101

Peach-Mango Soup, 205

Potato Soup, 101

Vegetables & Sides

Arancini di Riso, 193

Bean Salad, 113

Caponata Ai Capperi, 139

Carciofi Ripieni , 67

Eggplant Parmesan, 29

Eggplant Relish, 139

Fiori Zucca Fritti, 51

Fried Zucchini Flowers, 51

Melanzane Sott'Aceto, 197

Micheline's Italian Potato Salad, 87

Micheline's Meatballs, 161

Patata Crocchetta, 165

Pickled Eggplant, 197

Potato Croquette, 165

Risotto, 107

Sal's Portobello Mushrooms, 19

Sautéed Escarole with garlic, 39

Squash & Apple Casserole, 31

Stuffed Artichokes, 67

Stuffed Risotto Balls, 193

Proof

Made in the USA
Charleston, SC
11 September 2015

46232067R00140